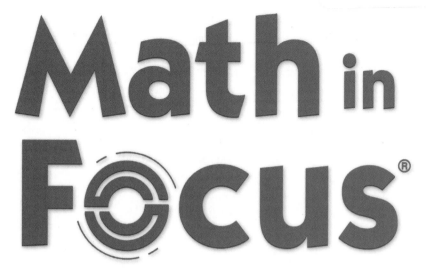

Math in Focus®

Singapore Math®
by Marshall Cavendish

Extra Practice and Homework

Program Consultant
Dr. Fong Ho Kheong

Marshall Cavendish
Education

U.S. Distributor

Houghton Mifflin Harcourt.
The Learning Company™

Course
3B

© 2020 Marshall Cavendish Education Pte Ltd

Published by Marshall Cavendish Education
Times Centre, 1 New Industrial Road, Singapore 536196
Customer Service Hotline: (65) 6213 9688
US Office Tel: (1-914) 332 8888 | Fax: (1-914) 332 8882
E-mail: cs@mceducation.com
Website: www.mceducation.com

Distributed by
Houghton Mifflin Harcourt
125 High Street
Boston, MA 02110
Tel: 617-351-5000
Website: www.hmhco.com/programs/math-in-focus

First published 2020

ISBN 978-0-358-10313-4

Printed in Singapore

2 3 4 5 6 7 8 9   1401   26 25 24 23 22
4500840184   B C D E F

The cover image shows a rockhopper penguin.
Rockhopper penguins live in the cold waters of South America, South Africa, and Antarctica. They feed on small fish, krill, or squid. A unique characteristic is the yellow crest on their heads. They are amazing swimmers, but are also very agile on land, getting their name from the way they leap effortlessly over rocks. There are no distinct differences in physical characteristics between the males and females so a DNA test is required to check the gender of a rockhopper penguin.

Contents

Preface

Math in Focus®: *Extra Practice and Homework* is written to complement the Student Edition in your learning journey.

The book provides carefully constructed activities and problems that parallel what you have learned in the Student Edition.

- **Activities** are designed to help you achieve proficiency in the math concepts and to develop confidence in your mathematical abilities.

- **MATH JOURNAL** is included to provide you with opportunities to reflect on the learning in the chapter.

- **PUT ON YOUR THINKING CAP!** allows you to improve your critical thinking and problem-solving skills, as well as to be challenged as you solve problems in novel ways.

You may use a calculator whenever  appears.

BLANK

Name: _____ Date: _____

Chapter 7 Extra Practice and Homework
Functions

Activity 1 Understanding Relations and Functions

Given the relation described, identify the input and the output.

1 Chase wants to know his weekly salary when he works for a certain number of hours per week at a constant hourly pay rate.

2 Mr. Morris wants to know how many miles he can drive his car for when the fuel tank is filled with various gallons of gasoline.

Identify the type of relation between the inputs and the outputs.

3

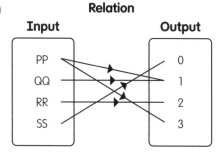

The relation between the inputs and the outputs is a _____ -to- _____ relation.

4

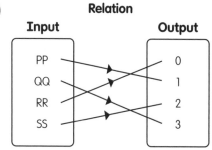

The relation between the inputs and the outputs is a _____ -to- _____ relation.

Solve.

5 The table shows the favorite color of each student in a class. Draw a mapping diagram to represent the relation between the favorite color and the number of students. Identify the type of relation between the favorite color and the number of students.

Input, Favorite Colors	Red	Blue	Yellow	Violet	Green
Output, Number of Students	6	10	3	3	3

6 The table shows the number of signatures collected each day for seven days by a citizen wanting to run for town council.

Input, Number of Signatures	55	43	55	30	75	55	62
Output, Day	1	2	3	4	5	6	7

Draw a mapping diagram to represent the relation between the number of signatures collected on each day. Identify the type of relation between the number of signatures and the day.

Identify the type of relation represented by each mapping diagram. Determine whether the relation is a function. Explain.

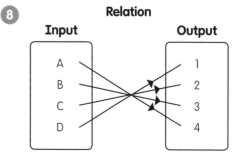

7 Relation

Input   Output

A   1
B   2
C   3
D   4

8 Relation

Input   Output

A   1
B   2
C   3
D   4

State whether each statement is True or False. Explain.

9 A one-to-one relation is always a function.

10 A function is a special type of relation.

11 When Melanie clicks on any of the icons in a folder on her computer, it will open only the file that she clicks on. She says the folder represents a function.

12 In a relation where the input is the age of the students in a class and the output is the height of the students, the relation is a function.

Solve.

13 The table shows the number of available parking spots in each of the five parking garages.

Input, Garage	A	B	C	D	E
Output, Number of Available Parking Spots	425	510	418	425	608

a Draw a mapping diagram to represent the relation between each garage and the number of available parking spots.

b From the mapping diagram, identify the relation between the garages and the number available parking spots.

c Determine whether the relation represented by the mapping diagram is a function. Explain.

14 The table shows the number of shoes produced by each of five factories and the production cost incurred during the week.

Factory	A	B	C	D	E
Number of Shoes Produced	674	480	535	605	674
Production Cost	$10,110	$7,200	$8,025	$9,075	$10,110

a Draw a mapping diagram to represent the relation between the factories and the number of shoes produced.

b From the mapping diagram, identify the relation between the factory and the number of shoes produced. Then tell whether the relation represented by the mapping diagram is a function. Explain.

c Draw a mapping diagram to represent the relation between the production costs incurred by the factories and the number of shoes produced. Identify the relation between the production cost and the number of shoes produced. Then tell whether the relation represented by the mapping diagram is a function. Explain.

Which of these graphs represents a function? Explain.

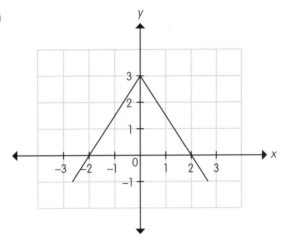

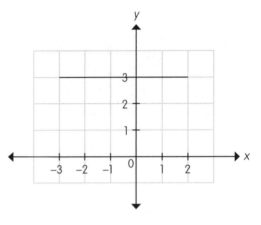

17

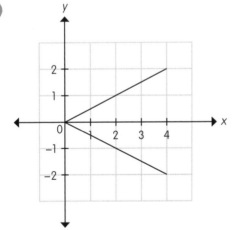

18

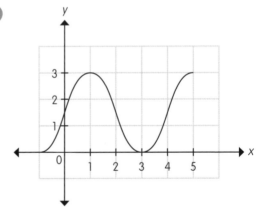

Chapter 7

Extra Practice and Homework
Functions

Activity 2   Representing Functions

Give a verbal description of each function. Then write an equation to represent the function.

1 Faith can type 75 words per minute on a computer keyboard. The number of words she can type, N, is a function of the amount of time, t minutes, she spends at the computer keyboard.

2 When Isabella goes on vacation, she boards her dog at a kennel. The kennel charges a flat fee of $50 and a daily rate of $10. The total amount Isabella pays for her dog to stay at the kennel, y dollars, is a function of the number of days that she boards the dog, d.

3 A dancing studio charges a $35 registration fee for class enrollment. The dance class Maria plans to take is $70 per hour. The total cost, y dollars, is a function of the number of class hours, x.

Write an equation to represent each function. Then construct a table of values to represent the function. Use values of _x_ from 1 to 3.

4 Morgan and her friends are making beaded bracelets to raise funds for a charity. Each bracelet is made up of 12 beads. The total number of beads needed, _y_, is a function of the number of bracelets they make, _x_.

5 A tank contains 72 gallons of water. A pump rated at 5 gallons per minute, is used to transfer water from the tank to a mixing vessel. The amount of water in the tank, _A_, is a function of the amount of time the pump is in use, _x_ minutes.

Each of these graphs represents a function. Find an equation to represent each function.

6

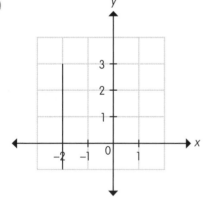

7

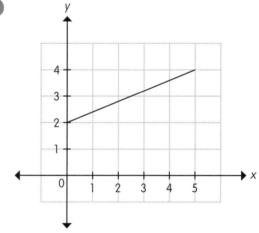

Solve.

8 The number of sheets of paper, *y*, remaining in the input paper tray of a photocopy machine is a function of the time, *x* minutes, the machine is operational. Initially, there are 360 sheets of paper in the tray. The number of sheets of paper decreases by 90 every minute.

a Give a verbal description of the function.

b Write an equation to represent the function.

c Construct a table of values to represent the function. Use values of *x* from 0 to 3.

d Graph the function on the coordinate plane below.

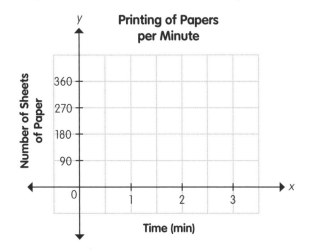

9 Ryan has a prepaid movie card with a value of $45. Every time he watches a movie, $7.50 is deducted from the value of his card. The amount of money remaining on his card, *y* dollars, is a function of the number of movies he watches, *x*.

a Give a verbal description of the function and then write an equation to represent the function.

b Construct a table of values to represent the function in **a**. Use values of *x* from 0 to 6.

c Use the table of values in **b** to graph the function on the coordinate plane below. Use 1 grid square on the horizontal axis to represent 1 movie watched for the *x* interval from 0 to 6 and 1 grid square on the vertical axis to represent $5 for the *y* interval from 0 to 50.

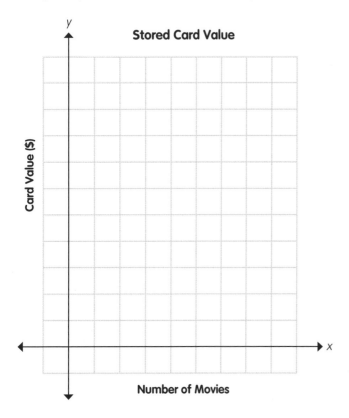

Stored Card Value

Card Value ($)

Number of Movies

Chapter 7

Extra Practice and Homework
Functions

Activity 3   Understanding Linear and Nonlinear Functions

Determine whether each table of values represents a linear or nonlinear function. Find the rate of change for each linear function.

1

x	1	3	5	7
y	2	18	50	98

2

x	−1	3	7	11
y	−4	8	20	32

3

x	−4	0	4	8
y	4	5	6	7

4

x	−2	0	2	4
y	8	4	−8	−14

State whether each graph represents a linear or nonlinear function. Find the rate of change for each linear function.

5

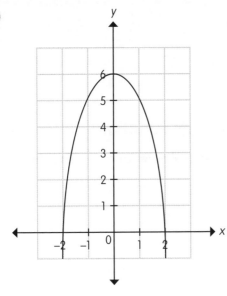

6

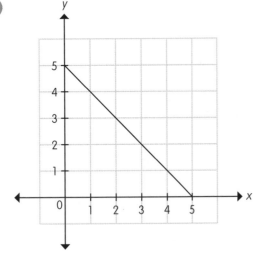

State whether each graph represents a linear or nonlinear function. State whether the function is increasing or decreasing.

 7

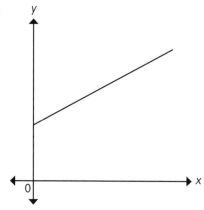

 8

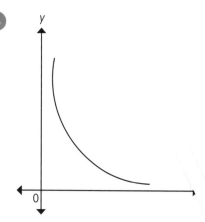

9

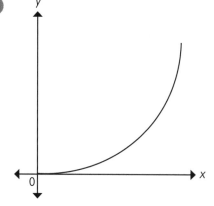

10

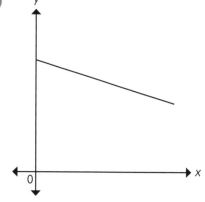

Solve.

11 A hot beverage dispenser machine with a capacity of 3.3 liters dispenses 110 milliliters for every press of the dispense button. The total amount of the beverage left in the dispenser, V liters, is a function of the number of presses on the dispense button, p.

a What is the least possible input and the corresponding output value? Explain.

b Is the function linear or nonlinear? Explain.

c Sketch a graph for the function.

12 A cell undergoes cell division and splits into 2 cells in an hour. Each cell continues to split into 2 cells every hour. The total number of cells, N, is a function of the time taken for cell division, t.

  a Is the function linear or nonlinear. Explain.

  b Sketch a graph for the function.

13 Jenna had $24 at first. She saved $8 each day. The amount of money, y dollars, she saved is a function of the number of days, x days, she took to save.

a Is the function linear or nonlinear? Is the function increasing or decreasing?

b Sketch the graph of the function.

Chapter 7

Extra Practice and Homework
Functions

Activity 4   Comparing Two Functions

Solve.

1   Determine whether the equation $y = \frac{5}{2}x - 3$ can represent the tables of values in **a** and **b**, and the graphs in **c** and **d**.

a

x	−2	0	2	4
y	8	3	−2	13

b

x	−2	0	2	4
y	−8	−3	2	7

c

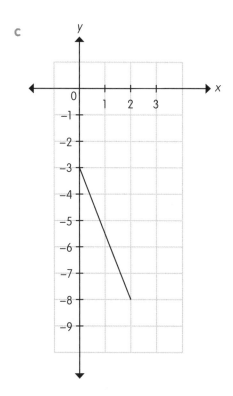

d

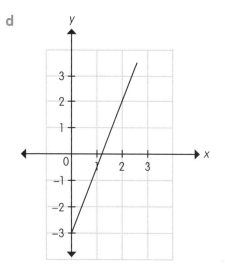

2 Determine whether the table of values can represent the equations in **a** and **b**.

x	−1	2	5
y	7	−5	−17

a $y = 4x - 3$ \qquad\qquad\qquad\qquad **b** $y = -4x + 3$

3 Determine whether the graph can represent the table of values.

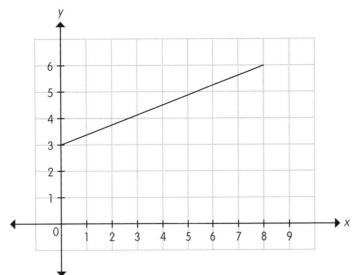

x	0	4	8
y	3	5	7

4 Determine whether the verbal description can represent the equation in **a** and **b**, and the table of values in **c**.

Maya has 50 stamps in her collection. When she joins a philatelic club, she receives 12 stamps every month from the club. y represents the total number of stamps she has and x represents the number of months.

a $y = 50 + 12x$ \qquad\qquad\qquad\qquad **b** $y = 12 + 50x$

c

Number of Months (x)	3	7	11
Total Number of Stamps (y)	86	134	182

5 Two identical water tanks A and B contain some water. Water is added to each tank by way of dedicated water faucets. The functions that relate each tank's total volume of water, V gallons, to the number of minutes, t, that each faucet is running, are as follows:

Tank A: $V = 80 + 25t$
Tank B: $V = 100 + 15t$

a Interpret and compare the rates of change of two functions.

b Graph the two functions on the same coordinate plane for the first 6 minutes. Use 1 grid square on the horizontal axis to represent 1 minute for the x interval from 0 to 6 and 1 grid square on the vertical axis to represent 25 gallons for the y axis from 25 to 250.

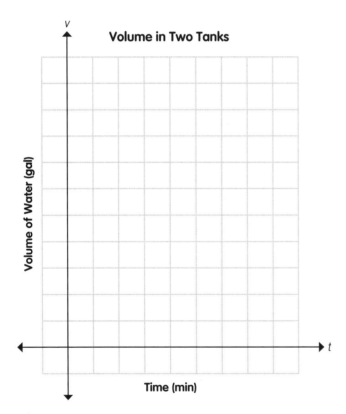

Volume in Two Tanks

Volume of Water (gal)

Time (min)

c Which tank is most likely to be filled to capacity first? Explain.

6 You have two options of paying for a lawn service for your backyard. Both options involve paying a flat fee and then paying an additional hourly charge for labor. For each function, the total amount you would pay, y dollars, is a function of the number of hours worked, t.

Option A

Number of Hours Worked (t)	0	2	4
Total Fee (y dollars)	25	45	65

Option B   A basic rate of $20 plus $12 per hour

a Find an equation to represent each function.

b A worker is employed for the lawn service for 8 hours. Which option is better for the worker? Explain.

Name: _____ Date: _____

Mathematical Habit 2 Use mathematical reasoning

Haley says that the graph shown is a function.

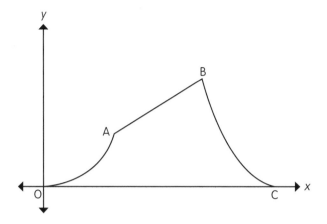

Describe the relationship between x and y for each section, OA, AB, and BC. Hence, explain whether Haley is correct.

Mathematical Habit 4 Use mathematical models

The owner of a baseball team hires a firm to produce inspirational posters to commemorate their 10th championship title. The firm charges a basic fee of $500 and an additional $2.50 for each poster produced. The cost, C dollars, is a function of the number of posters produced, p.

a Write an equation to represent the function, C.

b Graph the function in a. Use 1 grid square on the horizontal axis to represent 100 posters for the x interval from 0 to 600 and 2 grid squares on the vertical axis to represent $500 for the y axis from 0 to 2,000.

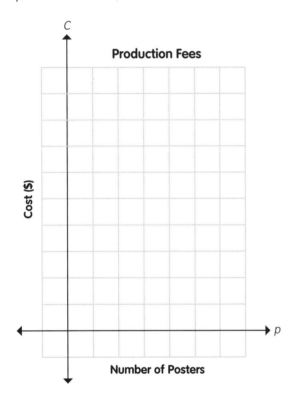

c The owner of the baseball team plans to sell the posters during the next game for $4 each. The profit, P dollars, is a function of the number of posters sold, p. Given that profit is the difference between revenue received from the sale of p posters and the cost of producing p posters, write an equation to represent the function P.

Extra Practice and Homework
The Pythagorean Theorem

Activity 1   Understanding the Pythagorean Theorem and Plane Figures

 Identify and shade two different right triangles in each figure and draw an arrow pointing at the hypotenuse.

1

2

Find the value of x in each triangle.

 3

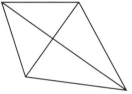

x cm

7 cm

24 cm

4

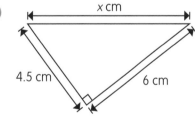

x cm

4.5 cm

6 cm

5

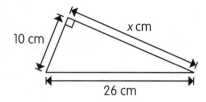

10 cm

x cm

26 cm

6

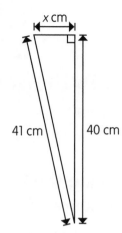

x cm

41 cm

40 cm

Find the value of *x* and of *y* in each triangle. Round non-exact answers to the nearest tenth.

7

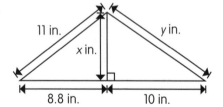

11 in.

y in.

x in.

8.8 in.

10 in.

8

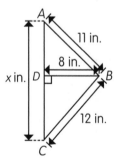

A

11 in.

8 in.

x in. *D*

B

12 in.

C

9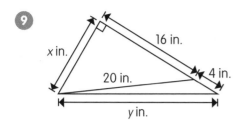

10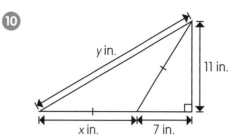

 Solve. Round non-exact answers to the nearest tenth.

11 Alex placed a 12-foot ladder against a wall. The bottom of the ladder was 5 feet away from the wall. Find the height of the wall.

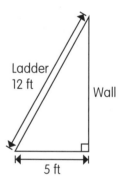

12 One end of a cable is attached to the top of a flagpole and the other end is attached 6 feet away from the base of the pole. The height of the flagpole is 12 feet. Find the length of the cable.

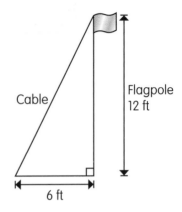

13 An escalator runs from the first floor of a shopping mall to the second floor. The length of the escalator is 32 feet and the distance between the floors is 15 feet. Find the distance from the base of the escalator to the point on the first floor directly below the top of the escalator.

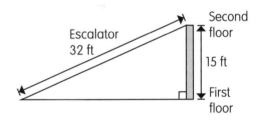

14 A hot air balloon is attached to the ground by a taut 100-meter cable, as shown in the diagram. Find the vertical height of the balloon above the ground.

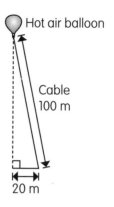

15 A taut cable connects two cable car stations A and B which are positioned 50 meters and 20 meters above the ground. The horizontal distance between the stations is $\frac{1}{2}$ kilometer. Find the length of the cable.

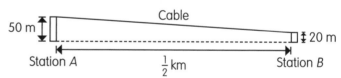

16 Sono Road runs from South to North and Ewest Road runs from East to West intersecting at point X. Jake and Ling are at point P on Sono Road 30 meters from point X. Jake walks along Sono Road to point X then turns east and walks 20 meters to point Q on Ewest Road. Ling walks on a path linking point P to point Q. Find the difference in distance between the two routes.

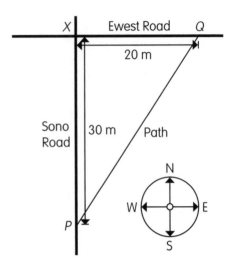

17 A 15-foot vertical pole has two strings of equal length attached to it at different points. The other end of one string, represented by $\overline{AB}$ in the diagram is tethered to the ground 12 feet from the base of the pole. The other end of the other string, represented by $\overline{CD}$ in the diagram is tethered to the ground 13 feet from the base of the pole.

a Find the length of the string.

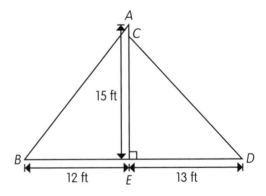

b Find the distance between the points A and C.

18 The diagonal of a square piece of cardboard is 28 inches.

a Find the perimeter of the square.

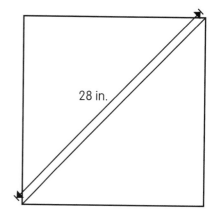

28 in.

b Find the area of the square.

19 Determine which field is a right triangle.

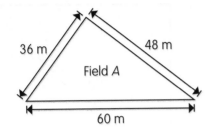

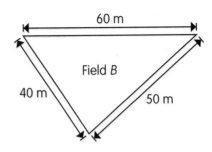

20 In the diagram, m∠ADB is 90°, AD is 22.6 inches, BC is 13 inches, and AB is 34.4 inches.

a Find the length of $\overline{AC}$.

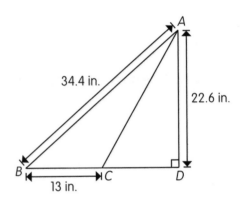

b Find the area of triangle ACD.

21 A whiteboard is 6 feet long and 3 feet wide. Find the length of the longest straight line that can be drawn on the whiteboard.

22 Points *A*, *B*, and *C* are corners of a triangular field where m∠*ABC* is 90°, *AB* is 40 meters and *BC* is 45 meters.

a Find the length of $\overline{AC}$.

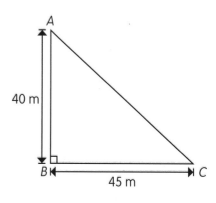

b John walks along the edge of the field from point *A* to point *C*. If *P* is the point on $\overline{AC}$ when John is nearest to point *B*, find the length of $\overline{BP}$.

23 A map with a scale of 1 : 50,000 shows the locations of four towns A, B, C, and D. On the map, the distance between Town A and Town B is 6 centimeters, the distance between Town B and Town C is 7 centimeters, and the distance between Town C and Town D is 8 centimeters. Given that m$\angle ABC$ = m$\angle ADC$ = 90°, find the actual distance between Town A and Town D.

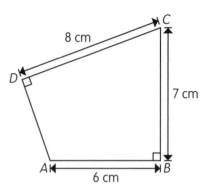

24 In the diagram, *AB* is 20 meters, *BC* is 65 meters, *CD* is 60 meters, *AD* is 16 meters, and *BD* is 25 meters. Determine if triangle *ABD* and triangle *BDC* are right triangles. Explain.

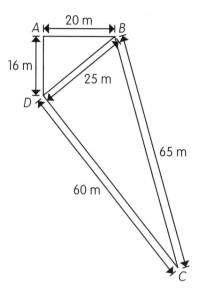

25 In rectangle *PQRT*, *PQ* is 80 feet, *QR* is 65 feet, *RS* is 30 feet, and m∠*SUP* is 90°.

a Find the perimeter of the shaded triangle.

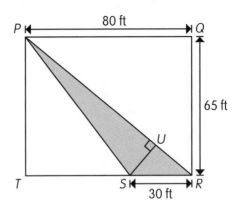

b Find the area of the shaded triangle.

c Find the length of $\overline{SU}$.

Chapter 8

Extra Practice and Homework
The Pythagorean Theorem

Activity 2   Understanding the Distance Formula

Solve.

1) Points $P(-4, 3)$ and $Q(4, -3)$ are plotted on a coordinate plane. Find the exact distance between points P and Q.

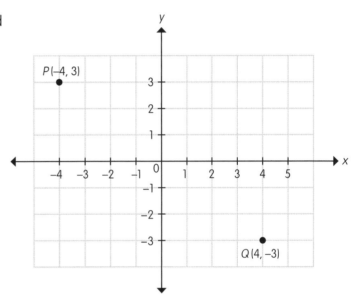

Find the distance between each pair of points. Round your answers to the nearest tenth, where applicable.

2 $A(3, -2)$, $B(0, -4)$

3 $C(4, 2)$, $D(2, -6)$

4 $E(3, -3)$, $F(-7, 8)$

5 $G(-1, -4)$, $H(-2, -5)$

6 Sara plots the points $P(-3, 4)$, $Q(3, 3)$, and $R(4, -3)$ on a coordinate plane. She joins the three points to form triangle PQR. Is the triangle an isosceles triangle? Explain.

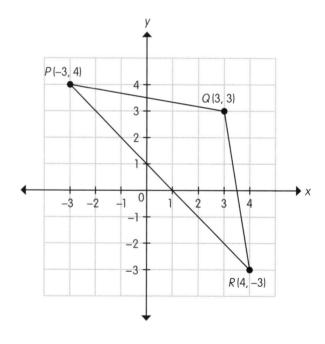

Use the data in the diagram for ⑦ to ⑨. Each unit on the grid equals 1 kilometer. Round your answers to the nearest tenth, where applicable.

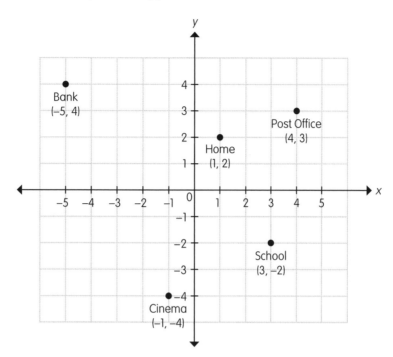

⑦ Find the approximate distance from Maria's home to each of the following locations.

a Bank

b School

c Post Office

d Cinema

8 Which locations are the same distance from Maria's home?

9 On a particular day, Maria traveled from her home to school. After school, she went to the post office to mail a letter. Then, she went home. Find the total distance she traveled.

Solve. Round your answers to the nearest tenth, where applicable.

10 Town *A* and Town *B* are located at the points shown in the diagram. Mr. Peterson wants to drive from Town *A* to Town *B*. He can choose between the route that takes him through Towns *P* and *Q*, or the route that takes him through Town *R*. Each unit on the grid equals 1 kilometer.

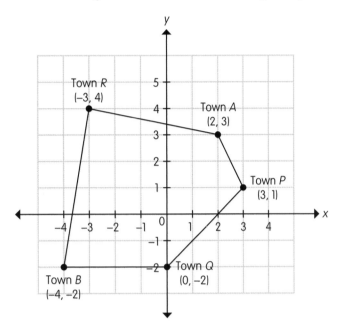

a Which is the shorter route?

b What is the difference in distances of the two routes?

11　The positions of a boat and a lighthouse are shown on the grids. Each unit on the grid equals $\frac{1}{2}$ mile.

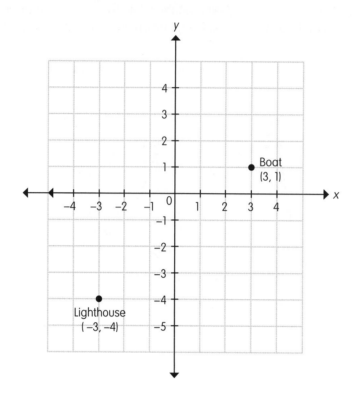

a　How far is the boat from the lighthouse?

b　The boat takes 20 minutes to travel to the lighthouse. Find the speed of the boat in miles per hour.

Chapter 8

Extra Practice and Homework
The Pythagorean Theorem

Activity 3   Understanding the Pythagorean Theorem and Solids

 Solve. Round non-exact answers to the nearest tenth, where applicable.

1 Find the values of x and of y in the triangular prism.

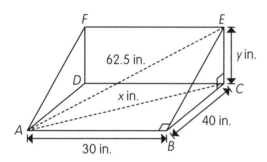

2 Find the values of x and of y in the rectangular prism.

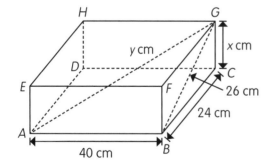

3 The diagram shows a cube of side 7 inches. Find the lengths of *AC* and of *AG*.

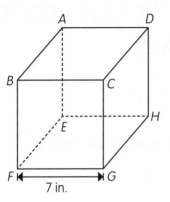

7 in.

4 The diagram shows a tent with triangular cross-section and a rectangular base, 10 meters by 8 meters. Its height is 3 meters. Find the lengths of *DM* and of *AF*.

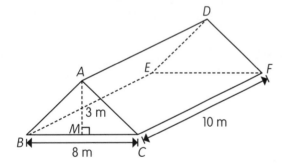

5 The diagram shows a prism with a square base *ABCD*. Its height is 30 inches and its diagonal *AG* is 50 inches. Find the length of *AB*.

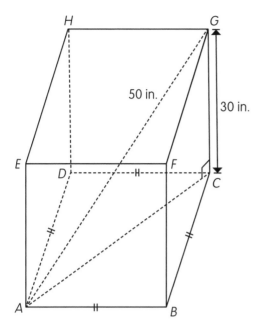

6. The diagram shows a rectangular room with length of 24 feet, width of 16 feet and height of 9 feet. A fly lands on the point M, midway between points H and G on the ceiling. Two spiders, A and B, are at corner A.

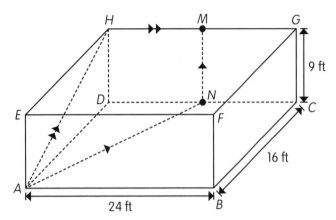

Spider A moves in a straight line from point A to point N, which is directly below point M. Then, it moves up to point M. Spider B moves in a straight line from point A to point H, and then horizontally to point M. If both spiders are moving at the same speed, which spider will get to the fly first?

Mathematical Habit 2 Use mathematical reasoning

The diagram shows a cube with side length of 10 inches.

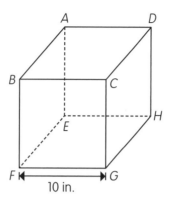

Luis thinks that the length of *AG* is the longest. Matt thinks that the length of *DF* is the longest. Who is correct? Explain.

Mathematical Habit 2 Use mathematical reasoning

Gavin plots the points C (4, 2), P (8, −10), Q (6, 8), R (−8, 6), and S (−8, −2). Using point C as the center of a circle, he draws a circle such that the circumference of the circle passes through three of the other points.

a Determine which point does **not** lie on the circumference of the circle. Explain.

b Does the point in a lie inside or outside the circle? Explain.

Chapter 9

Extra Practice and Homework
Geometric Transformations

Activity 1   Translations

Find the coordinates of the image under each translation.

1   *B* (3, −7) is translated by 2 units to the left and 8 units down.

2   *C* (8, −4) is translated by 6 units to the right and 7 units up.

On the coordinate plane, draw and label the images under each translation.

3   Alex's home is located at *H* (−3, 4). He uses the translations described in **a** to **d** to walk his dog.

  a From *H* (−3, 4), translate by 2 units to the left, 3 units down to *P*.

  b From *P*, translate by 6 units to the right, 3 units down to *Q*.

  c From *Q*, translate by 1 unit to the right, 5 units up to *R*.

  d From *R*, translate by 11 units to the left, 5 units down to *S*.

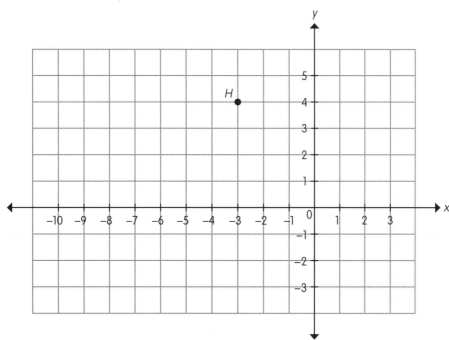

4 $\overline{DE}$ is translated 3 units to the left and 4 units up.

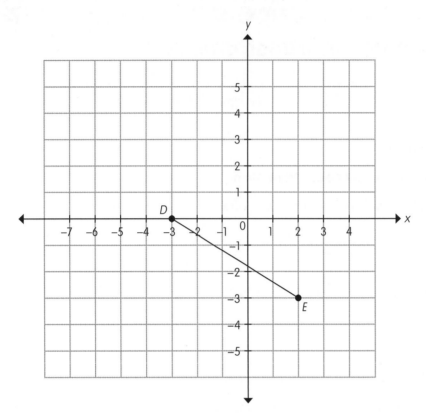

5 Triangle *FGH* is translated 4 units to the right and 3 units down.

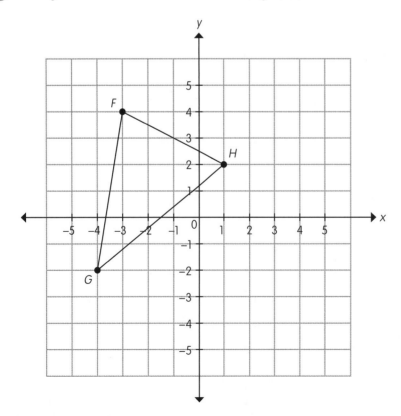

Solve.

6 A piece of plastic with vertices *A* (3, 2), *B* (2, 4), *C* (−1, 1) and *D* (4, −3) is moved by a translation to a new position *A'B'C'D'*. The coordinates of *A'* are (6, −1). Find the coordinates of the images of *B'*, *C'* and *D'*. Draw *A'B'C'D'* on the coordinate plane.

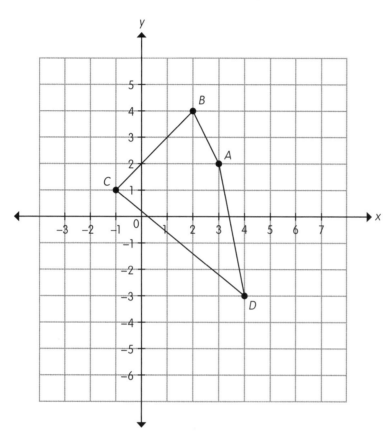

7 An object on the floor of a warehouse has a triangular base. Peter moved the object from its position at *ABC* under a translation that moves each point (*x, y*) to (*x* + 3, *y* − 2). Given *A* (−2, 3), *B* (2, 4), and *C* (7, −1), find the coordinates of *A'*, *B'*, and *C'*. Draw *ABC* and *A'B'C'* on the coordinate plane.

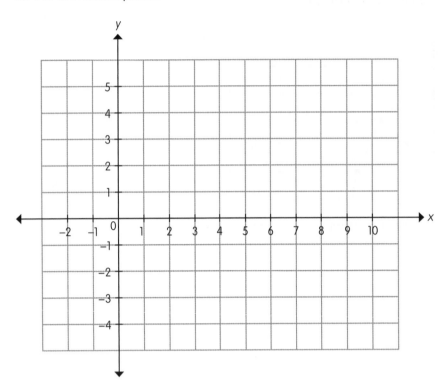

8 A computer program T guides a robot to move an object on the coordinate plane 5 units to the left and 3 units up. $\overline{AB}$ is translated by T to $\overline{A'B'}$. What are the coordinates of A and B given A' (7, 3) and B' (2, 1)?

9 A line has the equation $y = x - 3$. It is translated by 7 units down. What is the equation of the new line? How do the slopes of the line and its image compare?

10 On a coordinate plane, an object at $P(-2, 3)$ is copied by moving it to the point $P'(5, -1)$. Describe the translation of this point both verbally and algebraically.

Extra Practice and Homework
Geometric Transformations

Activity 2   Reflections

Draw and label the image.

1 Reflection in the *x*-axis

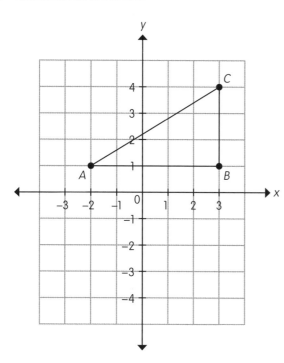

2 Reflection in the *y*-axis

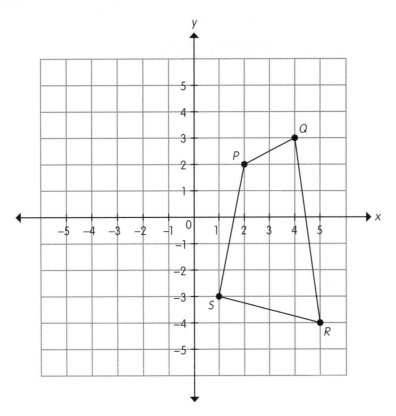

3 The positions of two sticks $\overline{AC}$ and $\overline{BD}$ are shown in the coordinate plane. Draw the images $\overline{A'C'}$ and $\overline{B'D'}$ with $y = 1$ as the line of reflection.

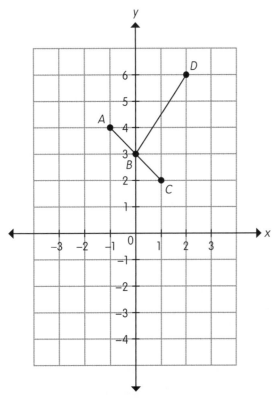

Solve.

4 Figure *ABCD* is drawn in the coordinate plane. It is repeated by first reflecting it in the *y*-axis to obtain the figure *A'B'C'D'*. The image is further repeated by reflecting it in the *x*-axis to obtain the figure *A"B"C"D"*.
Complete the table by finding the position of each of the other images.

Locations	Reflection in the y-axis	Reflection in the x-axis
A(–1, 3)	A'(___, ___)	A"(___, ___)
B(–3, 1)	B'(___, ___)	B"(___, ___)
C(–6, 1)	C'(___, ___)	C"(___, ___)
D(–6, 4)	D'(___, ___)	D"(___, ___)

Then, draw and label figure *ABCD* and the respective images on the coordinate plane.

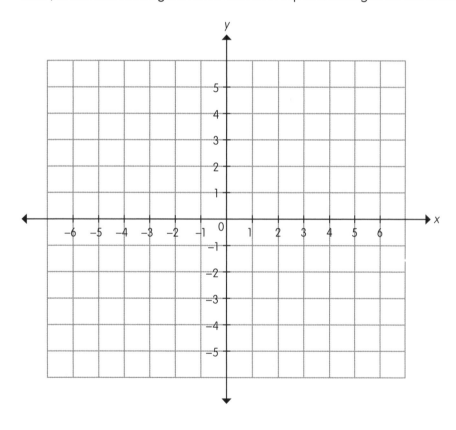

5 A graphic designer is drawing a logo in a coordinate plane. Some of the points are at A (−1, 5), B (−1, 3), C (−3, 1) and D (1, 1).

a Draw the line $x = 2$ on the same coordinate plane.

b The designer reflects the logo in the line $x = 2$. Draw $A'B'C'D'$ on the same coordinate plane.

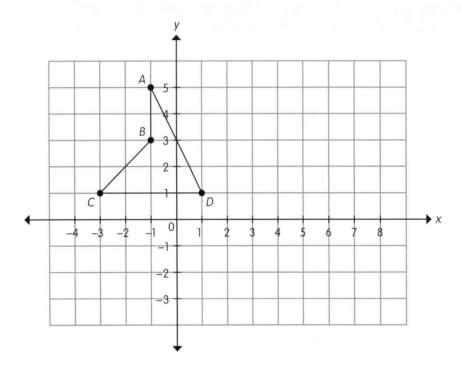

c What are the coordinates of A', B', C' and D'?

6 A symmetrical object, *ABCD*, is drawn in the coordinate plane. Three vertices of the object are at positions *A* (–3, 3), *B* (3, –3) and *C* (3, –5).

   a Draw and label points *A, B* and *C*.

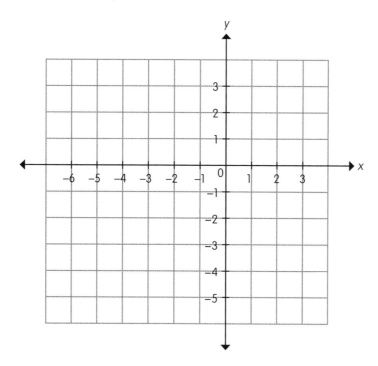

   b Point *B* is the reflection of point *A* in the line of symmetry. Find the equation of the line of symmetry.

   c Draw *ABCD* on the same coordinate plane given above. Find the coordinates of point *D*.

7 A kite has vertices *ABCD* with $\overline{BD}$ as its main diagonal. The positions of two of the vertices are *A* (2, 4) and *C* (−3, −1).

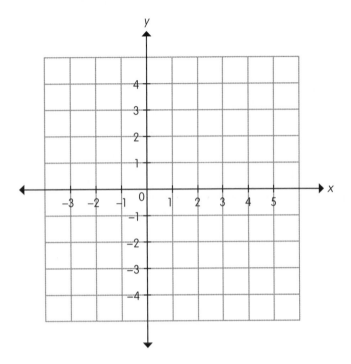

a Draw and label *A* and *C* in the coordinate plane.

b Find the equation of the main diagonal.

c A point *P* lies on the kite. It has coordinates *P* (4, −1). Find the coordinates of its image *Q* after a reflection in the diagonal $\overline{BD}$.

8 A figure *PQRS* in a coordinate plane is symmetrical about the line $y = 1 - x$. The vertex *Q* is the reflection of *P* in the line $y = 1 - x$.

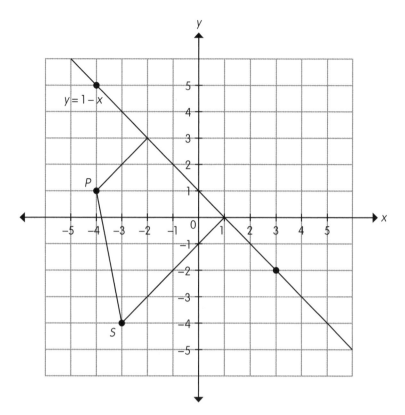

a The coordinates of *P* are (−4, 1). Draw and label point *Q*.

b The coordinates of *S* are (−3, −4). Find the coordinates of *R*.

c Describe the figure *PQRS*.

9 A figure *ABCD* in a coordinate plane is symmetrical about the line $y = 2x + 1$. The vertex *B* is the reflection of *A* in the line $y = 2x + 1$.

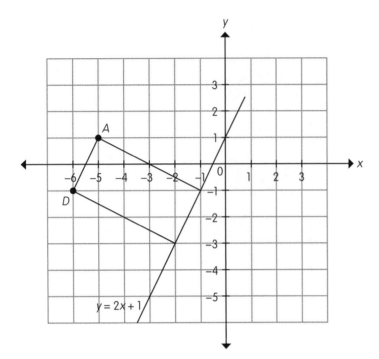

a The coordinates of *A* are (– 5, 1). Draw and label point *B*.

b The coordinates of *D* are (–6, –1). Draw and label point *C*.

c Describe the figure *ABCD*.

Chapter 9

Extra Practice and Homework
Geometric Transformations

Activity 3   Rotations

Solve.

1. A rotation of point *P* in the direction indicated about *O* maps *P* onto *P'*. State the angle of rotation.

   a Clockwise

   b Counterclockwise

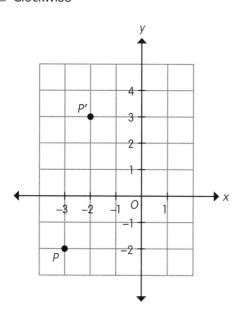

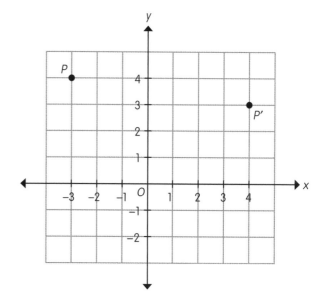

2 Each line has been rotated about the origin, O to form its image. State the angle and the direction of each rotation.

a

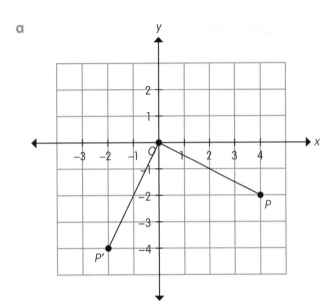

b

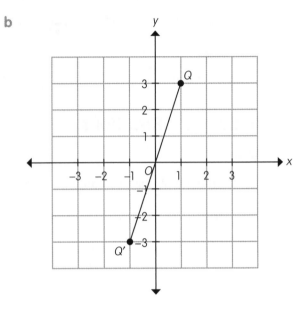

3 Pedro is in the seat of a Ferris wheel rotating about its center O. The seat is at a point P. He is rotated from P by each of the following rotations. Draw and label his positions after each rotation from P on the coordinate grid.

a A: clockwise rotation of 180°

b B: clockwise rotation of 270°

c C: counterclockwise rotation of 90°

d D: counterclockwise rotation of 45°

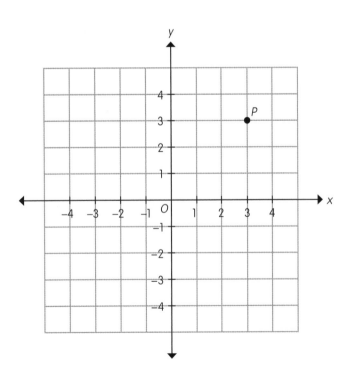

4 A spinner rotates about the center, O of a circular board. Initially, the spinner is in the position represented by $\overline{OP}$.

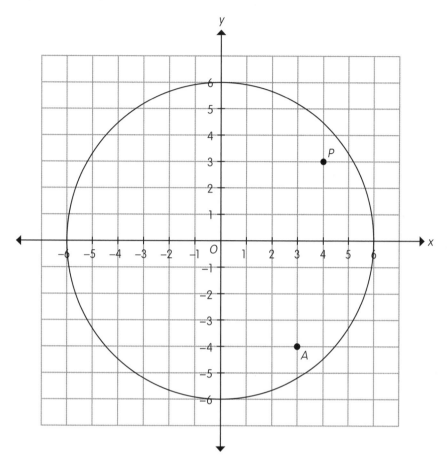

a The spinner rotates to the position represented by $\overline{OA}$. Describe the rotation.

b A point B (–3, 2) undergoes the same rotation. Find the coordinates of its image B'.

c A point C also undergoes the same rotation. Its image is C'(–1, –3). Find the coordinates of C.

5 The diagram shows the minute hand of a clock rotating about the center, *O* of the clock face. The minute hand is initially represented by $\overline{OP}$. Point *P* is at position (3, −4). Find the position of the minute hand under each of the following rotations.

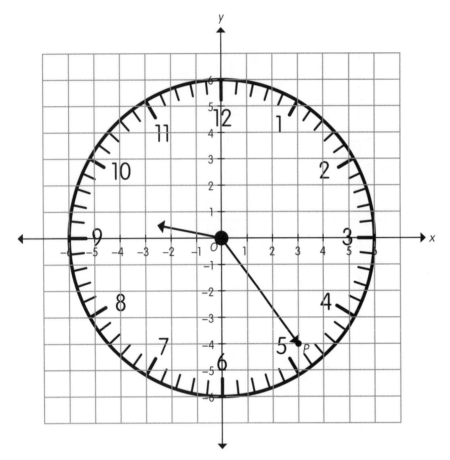

a Image *P'*: rotation of 90° counterclockwise

b Image *P''*: rotation of 90° clockwise

c Image *P'''*: rotation of 180° counterclockwise

6 A trapezoid, *ABCD*, is drawn on the coordinate plane.

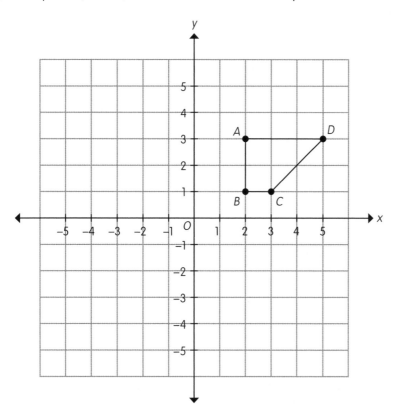

a *ABCD* is rotated 90° counterclockwise about the origin *O*. Draw and label the image of *A'B'C'D'*.

b What are the coordinates of *A'*, *B'*, *C'*, and *D'*?

c *ABCD* is rotated 180° clockwise about the origin, *O*. Draw and label the image of *A"B"C"D"*.

d Find the coordinates of *A"*, *B"*, *C"*, and *D"*.

e How are *A'B'C'D'* and *A"B"C"D"* related?

7 A regular pentagon *ABCDE* is rotated about its center *O*, so that its appearance stays the same, but the vertices are rotated to different positions. The pentagon is rotated so that the vertex *A* moves to the original position of *B*. Describe two possible rotations, stating each angle of rotation and the direction.

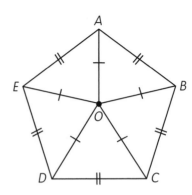

8 Triangle *OP'Q'* is the image of triangle *OPQ* under a rotation about *O*. State all possible invariant points. Explain.

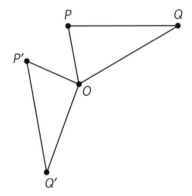

Extra Practice and Homework
Geometric Transformations

Activity 4   Dilations

Determine whether each transformation is a dilation. Explain.

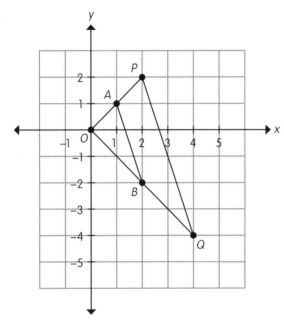

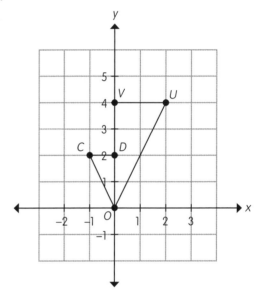

Solve.

3 Sofia has a triangle with side lengths of 3 inches, 4 inches, and 5 inches on a computer screen. She uses the computer to make some dilated copies of the triangle. Find the length of the sides of each copy with the scale factor given in **a** to **d**. In each case, state whether each copy is an enlargement or reduction of the original triangle.

a Scale factor: 3

b Scale factor: $\frac{1}{2}$

c Scale factor: 1.2

d Scale factor: 80%

4 Each figure is mapped onto its image by a dilation with its center at the origin, O. Draw each image.

a Scale factor 1.5

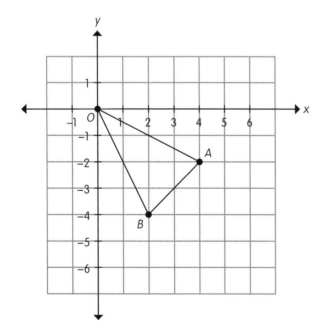

b Scale factor −1

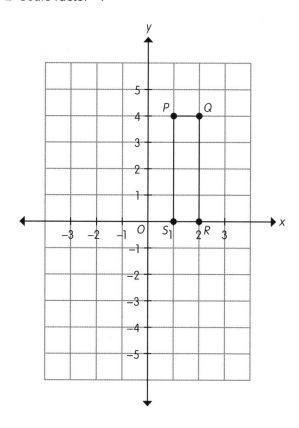

c Scale factor $-\dfrac{1}{2}$

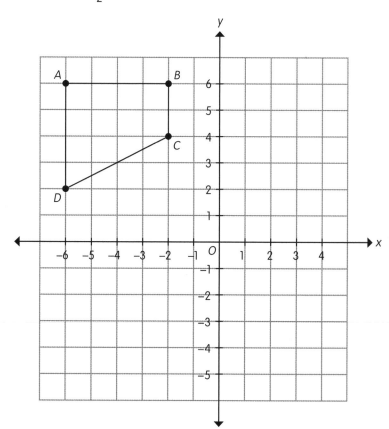

5 $\overline{PQ}$ is mapped onto $\overline{P'Q'}$ by a dilation with its center at the origin, *O*. The coordinates of *P'* are (–9, 6) and *Q'* are (0, 12). Find the scale factor.

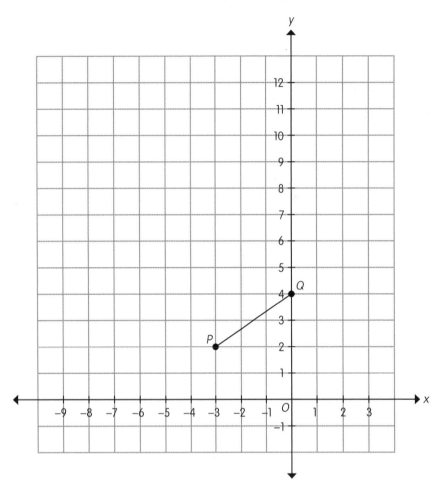

© 2020 Marshall Cavendish Education Pte Ltd

6 A circle, with radius 1 unit and center at $C(2, 3)$ is dilated to obtain a circle with radius 3 units and center at $C'(5, 4)$.

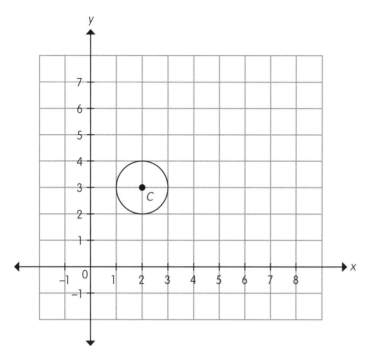

a Find the scale factor.

b Determine the center of dilation.

Draw the circle of radius 3 units with center C at $C'(5, 4)$ first before finding the center of dilation.

7 Triangle *ABC* is mapped onto its image triangle *A'B'C'* by a dilation. The coordinates are given in the table below.

Original Point	A (–2, 4)	B (–2, 0)	C (–1, 1)
Is Mapped Onto	A' (–5, 7)	B' (–5, –1)	C' (h, k)

a Draw triangle *ABC* on the coordinate plane. Mark and label points *A'* and *B'*.

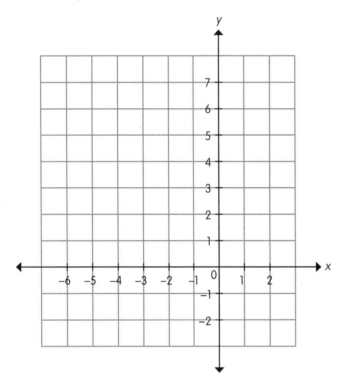

b Determine the coordinates of the center of dilation, *G*. Mark and label *G*.

c Find the scale factor.

d Find the values of *h* and *k*.

e Draw and label triangle *A'B'C'*.

8 Triangle *PQR* is mapped onto its image triangle *P'Q'R'* by a dilation. The respective coordinates are given in the table below.

Original Point	P (3, 0)	Q (2, 1)	R (h, k)
Is Mapped Onto	P' (5, 1)	Q' (3, 3)	R' (7, 3)

a Draw triangle *P'Q'R'* on the coordinate plane. Mark and label points *P* and *Q*.

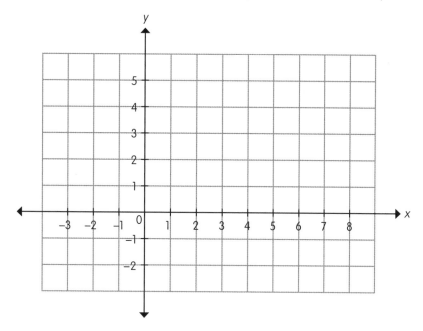

b Determine the coordinates of the center of dilation, *C*. Mark and label *C*.

c Find the scale factor.

d Find the values of *h* and *k*.

e Draw and label triangle *PQR*.

9 Triangle *ABC*, positioned at *A*(1, 1), *B*(2, 1) and *C*(2, 4), is mapped by a dilation of scale factor 2 about the origin, *O*, to obtain the image of triangle *A'B'C'*.

a Mark and label the positions of triangle *ABC* and triangle *A'B'C'* on the coordinate plane.

b Another dilation of scale factor –2 about the origin, *O*, maps triangle *ABC* onto triangle *A"B"C"*. Mark and label the position of triangle *A"B"C"*.

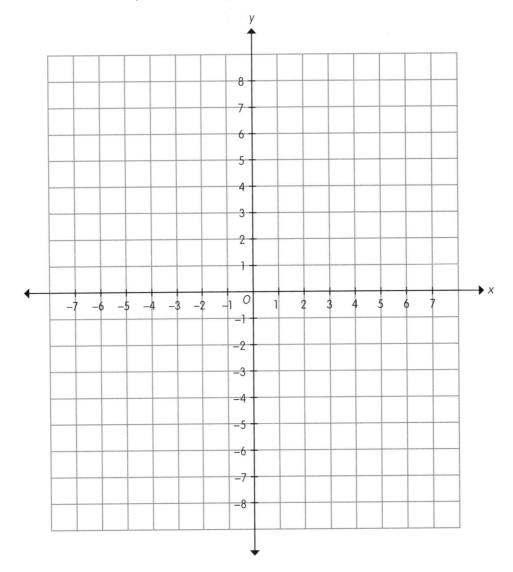

c Triangle *A'B'C'* can be mapped onto triangle *A"B"C"* by a single transformation in two ways. Describe each of the two ways.

Name: _____ Date: _____

Chapter 9

Extra Practice and Homework
Geometric Transformations

Activity 5 Comparing Transformations

Solve.

1 The diagram shows 3 triangles, *P, Q,* and *R* on a coordinate plane.

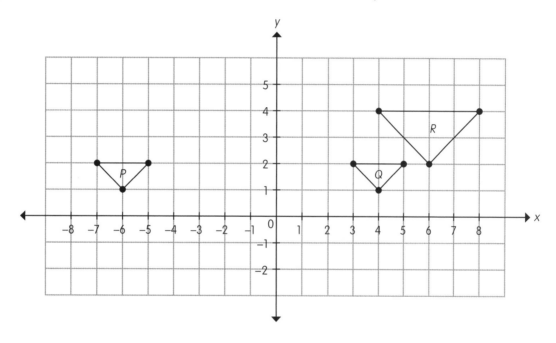

a Triangle *Q* can be mapped onto triangle *P* by a single transformation in two different ways. Describe each of the two ways.

b Describe the transformation that maps triangle *Q* onto triangle *R*.

2 A triangle with coordinates *A* (3, 1), *B* (4, 0), and *C* (5, 3) is drawn on the coordinate plane. Four other triangles are images of triangle *ABC* after each of the transformations in **a** to **d**.

  a △*ABC* is mapped onto △*DEF* by a translation of 6 units to the left. Draw △*DEF*.

  b △*ABC* is mapped onto △*GHI* by a reflection about the *x*-axis. Draw △*GHI*.

  c △*ABC* is mapped onto △*JKL* by a rotation of 180° about the origin, *O*. Draw △*JKL*.

  d △*ABC* is mapped onto △*PQR* by a dilation with center, *O*, and scale factor 2. Draw △*PQR*.

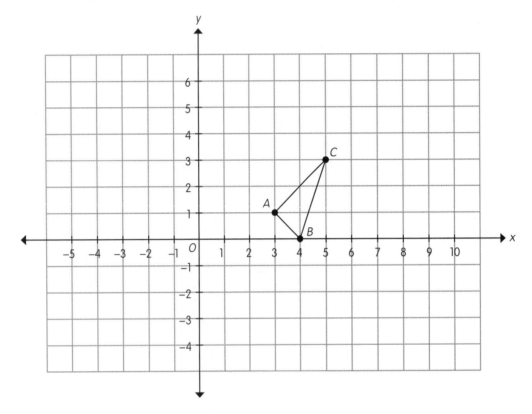

  e Which of the transformations result in images which are exactly the same shape and size as △*ABC*?

  f Which of the transformations results in images that have the same shape as △*ABC* but are of different sizes?

3 Quadrilateral *PQRS* with coordinates *P* (–1, 4), *Q* (–6, 3), *R* (–6, 1), and *S* (–3, 1) undergoes the following transformations.

a *PQRS* is mapped onto *P'Q'R'S'* by a reflection about the *y*-axis. Draw *P'Q'R'S'*.

b *PQRS* is mapped onto *P"Q"R"S"* by a reflection about the *x*-axis. Draw *P"Q"R"S"*.

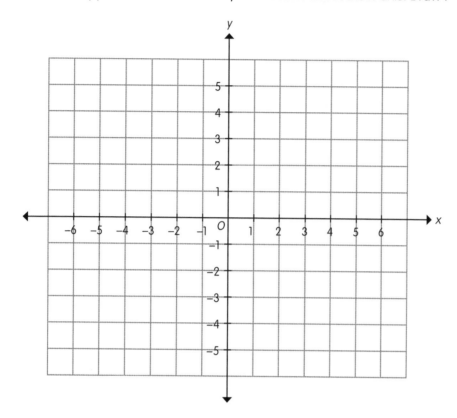

c *P'Q'R'S'* can be mapped onto *P"Q"R"S"* by a single transformation in two ways. Describe each of the two ways.

4 Refer to the diagram below. Four triangles are shown on the coordinate plane.

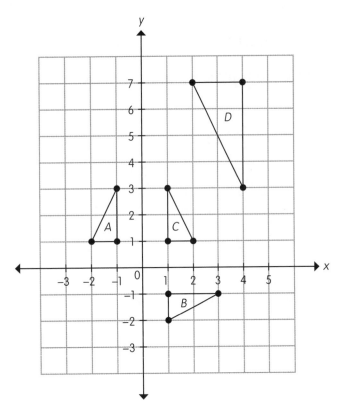

a Describe the transformation that maps △A onto △B.

b Describe the transformation that maps △B onto △C.

c Describe the transformation that maps △A onto △C.

d Describe the transformation that maps △C onto △D.

5 The table shows the coordinates for the vertices of four triangles.

ΔP	ΔQ	ΔR	ΔS
A (3, 4)	A′ (−1, −3)	A″(−1, −5)	A‴(−2, −7)
B (−1, 4)	B′ (3, −3)	B″(3, −5)	B‴(4, −7)
C (−1, 6)	C′ (3, −5)	C″(3, −3)	C‴(4, −4)

a Draw ΔP, ΔQ, ΔR, and ΔS.

b Describe two different single transformations that map ΔP onto ΔQ.

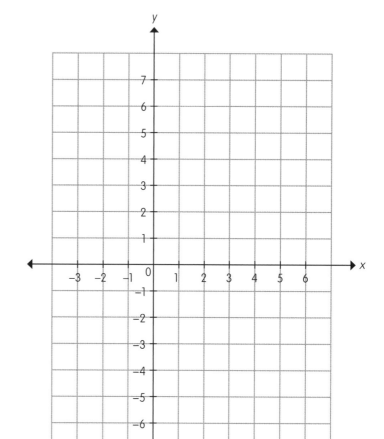

c Describe a transformation that maps ΔQ onto ΔR.

d Describe a transformation that maps ΔR onto ΔS.

6 The diagram shows a rhombus. Describe a single transformation (if any) or transformations that map the rhombus onto itself using each of the following:

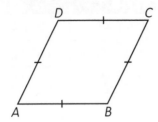

a Translation

b Reflection

c Rotation

d Dilation

Solve.

Mathematical Habit 5 Use tools strategically

Explain, without the use of a coordinate grid, how you would construct the line of reflection given that *P'* is the image of *P* under the reflection. Show your construction clearly. Then, explain how you would obtain the position of *Q'*, the image of *Q* in the same line of reflection.

Mathematical Habit 2 Use mathematical reasoning

The diagram show 2 pentagons A and B.

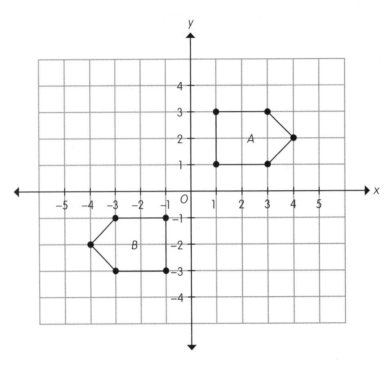

a Tara transforms pentagon A to pentagon B by using 2 reflections. Describe how Tara transforms pentagon A to pentagon B.

b Tim transforms pentagon A to pentagon B by using a translation, followed by a reflection. Describe how Tim transforms pentagon A to pentagon B.

Extra Practice and Homework
Congruence and Similarity

Activity 1 Understanding and Applying Congruent Figures

The given figures are congruent. Find the values of *p*, *q*, and *r*.

1

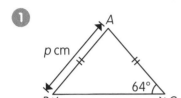

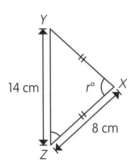

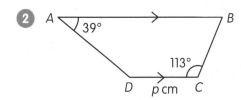

2

A   39°   B

113°

D   p cm   C

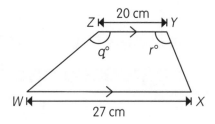

Z   20 cm   Y

q°   r°

W   27 cm   X

3

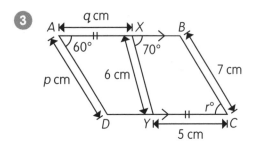

A   q cm   X   B

60°   70°

p cm   6 cm   7 cm

D   Y   r°   C

5 cm

Solve.

4 *ABCD* is a kite, whose diagonals intersect at *P*. Name all possible pairs of figures that are congruent. For each pair, name the corresponding congruent line segments and angles.

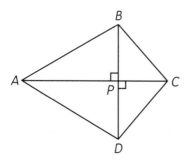

5 *ABCD* is a rhombus, whose diagonals intersect at *P*. Explain, using a test for congruent triangles, why △*PAB* ≅ △*PCD*.

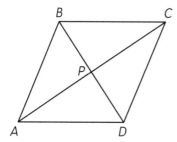

6 *ABCDEF* is a regular hexagon with diagonals $\overline{AC}$, $\overline{AD}$, and $\overline{AE}$ as shown. It is given that $\overline{AC}$ and $\overline{AE}$ are congruent diagonals.

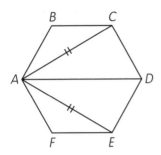

a Name two pairs of congruent triangles. For each pair, justify the congruency with a test for congruent triangles.

b Name a pair of congruent quadrilaterals.

7 In the diagram, *ABCD* is a rhombus and $\angle CDE = \angle ADE$.

a Identify two pairs of congruent triangles.

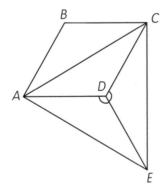

b For each pair in **a**, determine which congruence test proves that the triangles are congruent. Explain.

8 In the diagram, $\triangle ABC \cong \triangle DEC$. Find the values of u, v, w, x, y, and z.

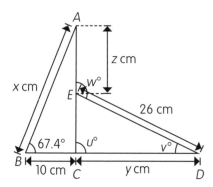

9 $ABCDE \cong QRSTP$. Find the values of u, v, w, x, and y.

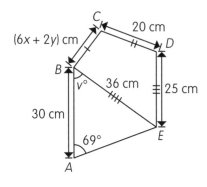 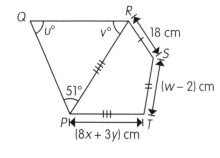

10 In the diagram, *ABDE* is a parallelogram. m∠*ACB* = m∠*DFE* = 90°.

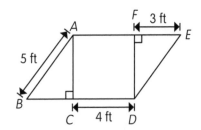

a Justify that △*ABC* ≅ △*DEF* with a test for congruent triangles.

b Write the congruence statement for a quadrilateral that is congruent to quadrilateral *ABDF*.

c Find the length of each side of the quadrilateral you named in **b**.

Extra Practice and Homework
Congruence and Similarity

Activity 2   Understanding and Applying Similar Figures

Identify the figures that seem similar. Explain your answer.

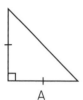

A   B   C   D   E

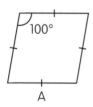
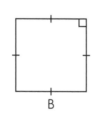
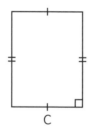

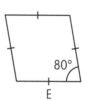

A   B   C   D   E

Solve.

3 Triangle *ABC* is similar to triangle *XYZ*. Find the scale factor by which △*ABC* is enlarged to △*XYZ*.

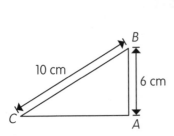 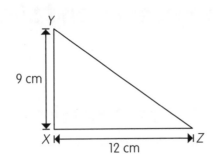

4 Triangle *ABC* is similar to triangle *XYZ*. Find the ratio of their areas.

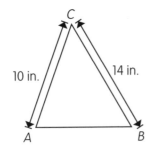 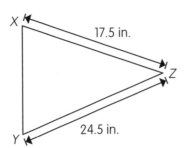

△ABC and △XYZ are similar. Find the value of *x* and of *y*.

5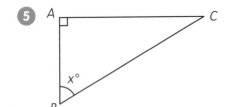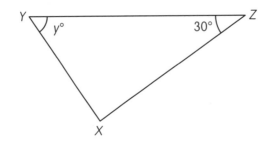

6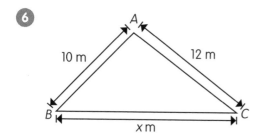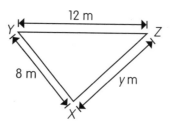

7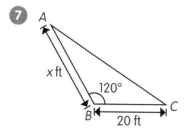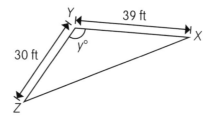

Solve.
ABCD and PQRS are similar. Find the value of p, q, and r.

8

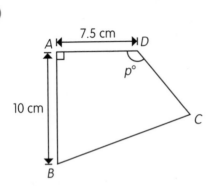

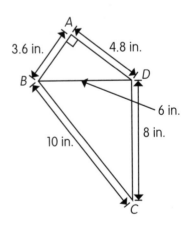

9 The figure consists of two similar triangles.

   a Write a statement of similarity of the two triangles.

   b Explain with a test why the triangles are similar.

10 The figure shows two similar triangles with m∠BAC = m∠CED.

a Write a statement of similarity of the two triangles.

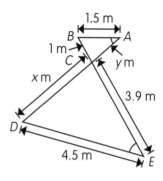

b Explain with a test why the triangles are similar.

c Find the values of unknowns, x and y.

11 The figure shows two similar triangles with $BE \parallel CD$.

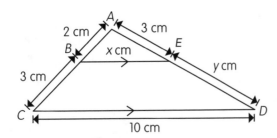

a Write a statement of similarity of the two triangles.

b Explain with a test why the triangles are similar.

c Find the values of the unknowns, x and y.

12 The figure shows two similar triangles with BA ∥ DE.

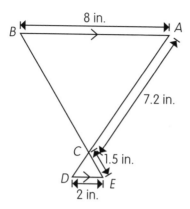

a Write a statement of similarity of the two triangles.

b Explain with a test why the triangles are similar.

c Find the lengths of $\overline{AD}$ and $\overline{BE}$.

13 The shape shown in Figure A consists of a circle, a square and an equilateral triangle. Figure B and Figure C are photocopies of Figure A.

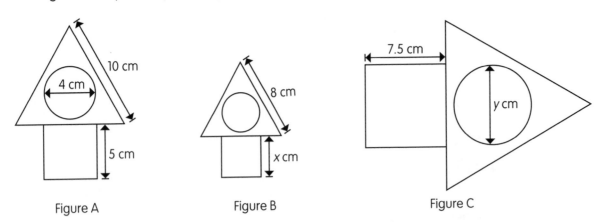

Figure A   Figure B   Figure C

a State whether Figure B and Figure C are enlargement or reduction of Figure A.

b In each case, find the scale factor.

c Find the values of the unknowns, x and y.

$\triangle XYZ$ is an enlarged copy of $\triangle ABC$.

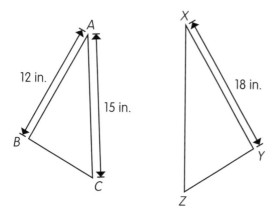

a Find the scale factor.

b Find the length of $\overline{XZ}$.

c The area of $\triangle ABC$ is 54 square inches. Find the area of $\triangle XYZ$.

15 In the figure, $PQ \parallel XY$.

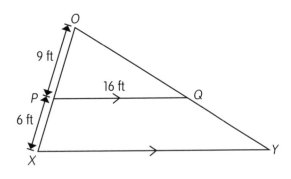

a Find the length of $\overline{XY}$.

b Find the ratio of the area of $\triangle OPQ$ to the area of the trapezoid $PQYX$.

c The area of $\triangle OPQ$ is 80 square feet. Find the area of trapezoid $PQYX$.

16 The diagram shows a triangular block with the inner triangle removed.

a Find the perimeter of the inner triangle removed.

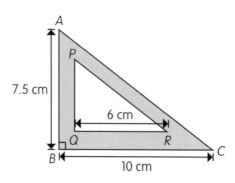

b Find the area of the remaining block.

17 Two vertical walls, $\overline{AP}$ and $\overline{BQ}$, are supported by poles $\overline{AQ}$ and $\overline{BP}$. Find the length of each pole and the distance between the walls, AB.

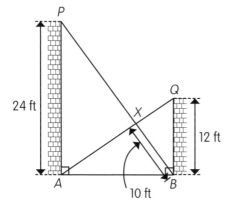

18 In the diagram, $AB \parallel CD \parallel EF$.

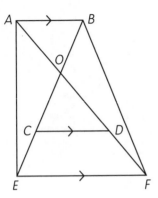

a Identify three pairs of similar triangles. For each pair, explain why they are similar.

b Is $\triangle AOE \sim \triangle BOF$? Explain.

Chapter 10

Extra Practice and Homework
Congruence and Similarity

Activity 3   Relating Congruent and Similar Figures to Geometric Transformations

State whether each figure and image are congruent or similar.

1 Rectangle *ABCD* is rotated 90° clockwise about vertex *A*.

2 A parallelogram is reflected in the *x*-axis and then reflected in the *y*-axis.

3 A photocopier dilates a picture by a scale factor of $\frac{3}{4}$.

4 A trapezoid is dilated with center (0, 0) and scale factor –1.

5 A hexagon is rotated 90° counterclockwise about its center (0, 0) and then dilated by a scale factor of 2.

6 △ABC is mapped onto △A'B'C' under a transformation. △A''B''C'' is the image of △A'B'C' under another transformation.

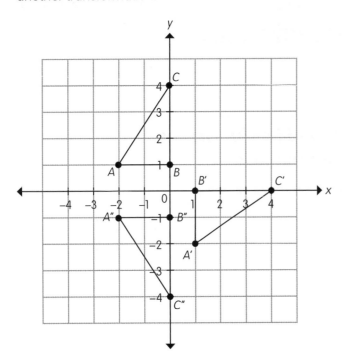

a Describe the transformations that map △ABC onto △A'B'C' and △A'B'C' onto △A''B''C''.

△ABC is mapped onto △A'B'C' by using a reflection in the line _____.

△A'B'C' is mapped onto △A''B''C'' by using a rotation of _____ about

the point (_____, _____).

b If the order of the transformations is reversed, draw $\triangle ABC$ and $\triangle A'B'C'$ and $\triangle A''B''C''$ on the coordinate plane below.

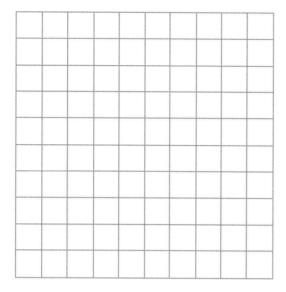

c Do the two triangles $\triangle A''B''C''$ have the same coordinates? Are they congruent? Explain.

3 Relating Congruent and Similar Figures to Geometric Transformations

Solve.

7 A triangle *ABC* with vertices *A* (–3, 4), *B* (–3, 2) and *C* (–6, 2) is reflected in the *y*-axis to obtain the image Δ*A'B'C'*. Δ*A'B'C'* is then mapped onto Δ*A"B"C"* shown in the diagram by another transformation.

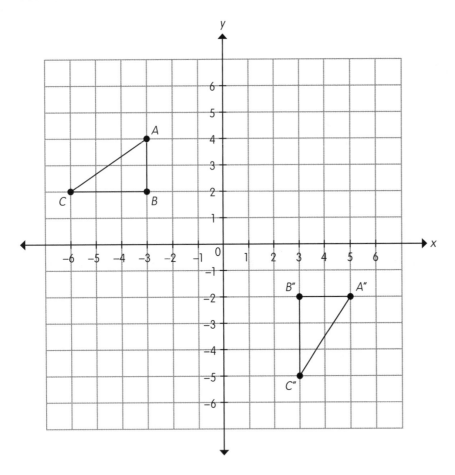

a Draw Δ*A'B'C'* on the same axes above.

b Describe the transformation that maps Δ*A'B'C'* onto Δ*A"B"C"*.

c Describe a single transformation that maps Δ*ABC* onto Δ*A"B"C"*.

8 A triangle *PQR* with vertices *P* (–2, 2), *Q* (–1, 3), and *R* (–1, 1) is dilated by a scale factor 2 with center *P* to obtain the image Δ*P'Q'R'*. Δ*P'Q'R'* is then mapped by another transformation onto Δ*P"Q"R"* shown in the diagram.

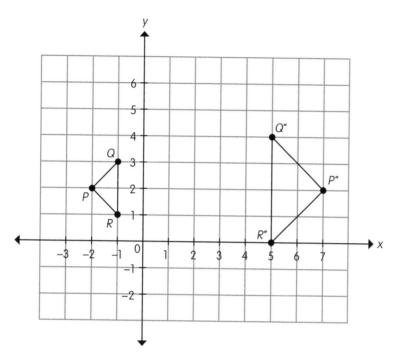

a Draw Δ*P'Q'R'* on the same axes above.

b Describe the transformations that maps Δ*P'Q'R'* on Δ*P"Q"R"*.

c Describe a sequence of transformations that maps Δ*PQR* onto Δ*P"Q"R"*.

9 △*ABC* is mapped onto △*A′B′C′* under a transformation. △*A′B′C′* is then mapped onto △*A″B″C″* under another transformation. Describe the sequence of transformations from △*ABC* to △*A″B″C″*.

a

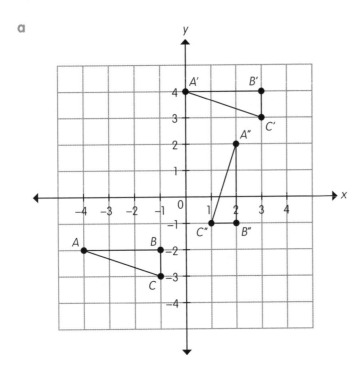

b

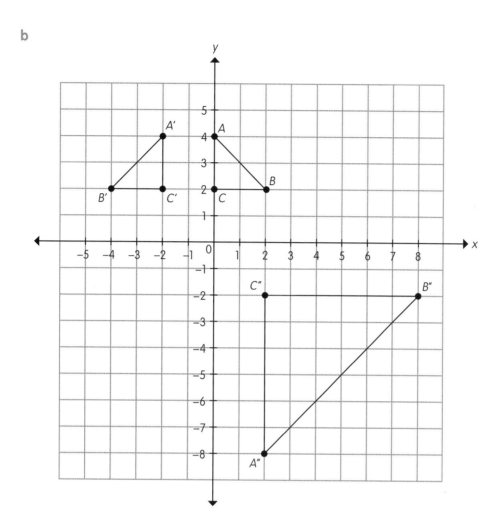

c

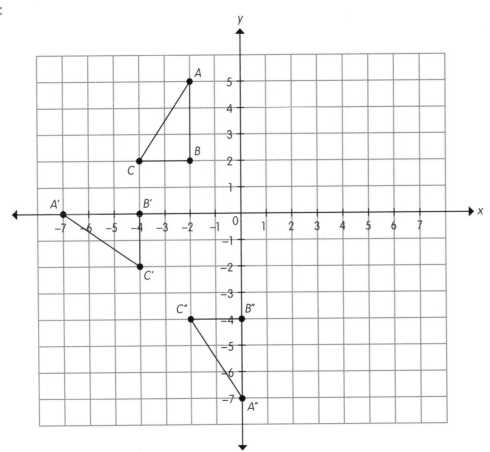

10 Quadrilateral *ABCD* is dilated with center *C* and scale factor 1.5. It is mapped onto *PQRS*. The length of $\overline{AB}$ is 3 feet and the area of *ABCD* is 12 square feet.

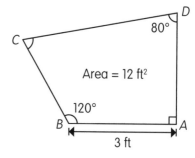

a Find m∠*QRS*.

b Find the length of $\overline{PQ}$.

c Determine the area of *PQRS*.

11. The area of a rectangular postcard is 60 square centimeters. A dilated copy has an area of 240 square centimeters. By what scale factor is the diagonal of the postcard enlarged?

Solve.

Mathematical Habit **4** Use mathematical models

Emma is 1.5 meters tall. She wants to find the height of a flagpole. Explain how she can find the height of the flagpole by adjusting her position from the flagpole and by measuring the length of her shadow in the early morning.

Mathematical Habit **1** **Persevere in solving problems**

Solve for *m* in terms of *n*.

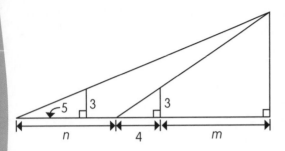

Use algebra to represent the height of the big triangle and solve.

Activity 1   Recognizing Cylinders, Cones, Spheres, and Pyramids

Write the name of the solid shape for each figure.

1

_____

2
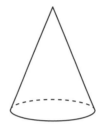

_____

3
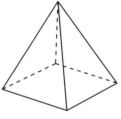

_____

4
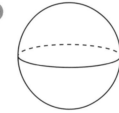

_____

5
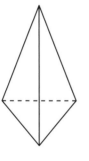

_____

6

_____

Write the name of the solid shape for each object.

 7

_____

8

_____

9

_____

10

_____

Identify and write the names of the solid shapes in the parts of each object.

11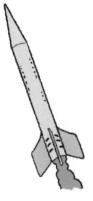

_____

12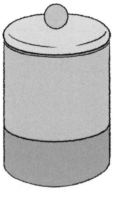

_____

Chapter 11

Extra Practice and Homework
Volume and Surface Area

Activity 2   Finding Volumes and Surface Areas of Cylinders

Use 3.14 as an approximation for π, unless stated otherwise. Round your answers to the nearest tenth where applicable.

Find the volume of each solid cylinder.

1

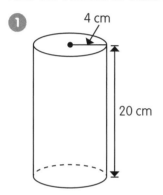

4 cm

20 cm

2

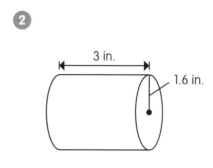

3 in.

1.6 in.

Solve.

3 The can has a diameter of 3.2 inches and a height of 7 inches.

   a What is the area of the base?

   b What is the area of the curved surface of the can?

   c What is the total surface area of the can?

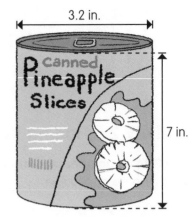

3.2 in.

7 in.

4 Nora wants to paint a plastic pen holder. She needs to paint the curved surface area and the base of the holder. What is the surface area she needs to paint?

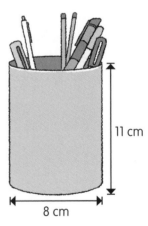

11 cm

8 cm

5 A cylindrical can has a capacity of 1,000 cubic inches. What is the height of the can if its radius is 5 inches?

6 An open cylinder has a diameter of 5 centimeters and a height of 20 centimeters. Find the surface area of the cylinder.

7 A cylindrical cup holds 500 cubic centimeters of water. The height of the cup is 10 centimeters. Calculate the diameter of the cup.

2 Finding Volumes and Surface Areas of Cylinders

8 A factory manufactures cylindrical cans. Each can has a volume of 240π cubic centimeters and a height of 15 centimeters.

a Find the diameter of each can.

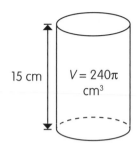

15 cm $V = 240\pi$ cm³

b The factory plans to manufacture a can with a height that is 20% shorter than the original can. What is the radius of the new can if the volume remains the same?

9 A cylindrical oil tank has a diameter of 16 inches and a height of 50 inches. The volume of oil in the tank is 1,920π cubic inches.

a What is the height of the oil in the tank?

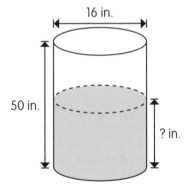

16 in.

50 in.   ? in.

b What percent of the tank is filled with oil?

Chapter 11

Extra Practice and Homework
Volume and Surface Area

Activity 3 Finding Volumes and Surface Areas of Pyramids and Cones

Use 3.14 as an approximation for π, unless stated otherwise. Round your answers to the nearest tenth where applicable.

Find the volume of each pyramid.

1

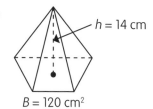

$h = 14$ cm

$B = 120$ cm²

2

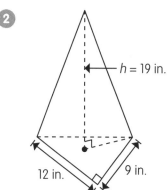

$h = 19$ in.

12 in.   9 in.

Find the volume and surface area of each cone.

3

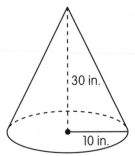

30 in.

10 in.

4

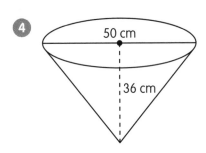

50 cm

36 cm

Solve.

5 A square pyramid has a volume of 4,000 cubic centimeters and a height of 30 centimeters.

    a What is the area of the square base of the pyramid?

    b What is the length of an edge of the base?

6 The volume of a pentagonal pyramid is 900 cubic inches. The area of the base of the pyramid is 270 square inches. What is the height of the pyramid?

7 A road construction marker in the shape of a cone has a slant height of 3.2 feet. If the curved surface area of the construction cone is 15 square feet, find the diameter of the cone.

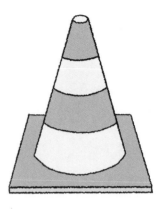

8 Cones A and B have the same height but different radii as shown in the diagram. If the volume of cone A is 0.72 cubic meters, find the volume of cone B.

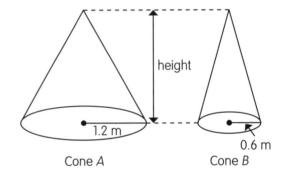

Cone A   Cone B

Chapter 11

Extra Practice and Homework
Volume and Surface Area

Activity 4   Finding Volumes and Surface Areas of Spheres

 Use 3.14 as an approximation for π, unless stated otherwise. Round your answers to the nearest tenth, where applicable.

Find the volume and surface area of each solid sphere.

1

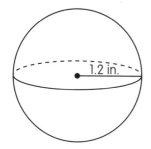

1.2 in.

2

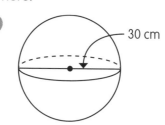

30 cm

Solve.

3 A globe is in the shape of a sphere. The diameter of the globe is 24 inches.

  a What is the surface area of the globe?

  b What is the volume of the globe?

4 Find the surface area of a sphere with a volume of 2,826 cubic inches.

5 The surface area of a ball is 28π square inches, what is the radius of the ball?

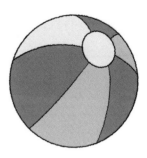

6 A bowl is in the shape of a hemisphere. The radius of the bowl is 12 centimeters. How many liters of water can the bowl hold?
(1,000 cm³ = 1 liter)

7 The flat surface of a solid hemisphere has a circumference of 25 centimeters.

a What is the radius of the hemisphere?

b What is the volume of the hemisphere?

c What is the total surface area of the solid hemisphere?

Chapter 11

Extra Practice and Homework
Volume and Surface Area

Activity 5   Real-World Problems: Composite Solids

Use 3.14 as an approximation for π, unless stated otherwise. Round non-exact answers to the nearest tenth, where applicable.

Solve.

1 A composite solid is made up of a cone joined to a cylinder as shown.

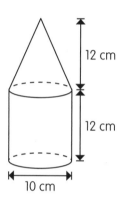

12 cm

12 cm

10 cm

   a What is the total surface area of the composite solid?

   b What is the volume of the composite solid?

2 The shape of a sausage is made up of two identical hemispheres attached to a cylinder. The length of the sausage is 5 inches and the diameter of the hemisphere is 0.6 inch. What is the volume of the sausage?

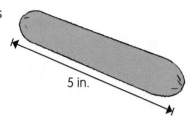

5 in.

3 A canvas tent is made of a cone whose base is mounted on the top of a cylinder as shown. The diameter of the cylinder is 6 meters and its height is 1.5 meters. The cone has a slant height of 5 meters. What is the total surface area of the tent?

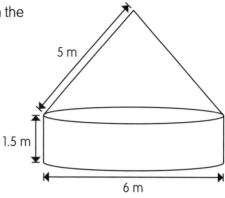

4 A pen holder is in the shape of a cube with a cylindrical hole through the middle. The edge length of the cube is 6 inches. The diameter of the cylindrical hole is 4.8 inches and its height is 4 inches.

a What is the volume of the pen holder?

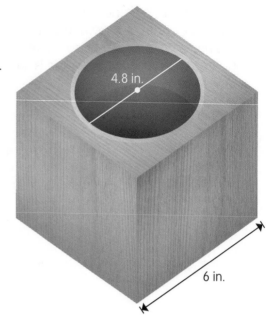

b What is the total surface area of the pen holder?

Mathematical Habit 2 Use mathematical reasoning

The diagram shows a solid cone in a cylinder without a lid.

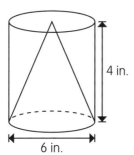

4 in.

6 in.

Ken says that the curved surface area of the cone is smaller than the curved surface area of the cylinder. Do you agree? Explain.

1 | **Mathematical Habit** **2** Use mathematical reasoning

Jake cuts a wedge, as shown by the dashed curve, from a cylinder of diameter 10 centimeters and height of 5 centimeters. What is the volume of the wedge in cubic centimeters?

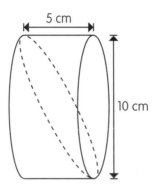

2 | **Mathematical Habit** **1** Persevere in solving problems

The net is made up of a square and four identical equilateral triangles. The length of the square is 6 inches. The net is folded to form a square pyramid. Find the volume of the pyramid.

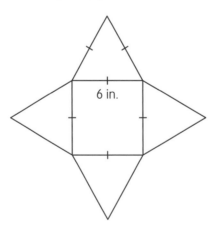

Chapter 12

Extra Practice and Homework
Statistics

Activity 1   Scatter Plots

On graph paper, construct a scatter plot for the given data.

1. Use 1 centimeter on the horizontal axis to represent 10 units. Use 1 centimeter on the vertical axis to represent 5 units.

x	20	30	70	80	70	10	60	50
y	10	16	36	40	12	7	30	28

x	40	60	30	70	40	50	40
y	21	31	18	37	20	26	22

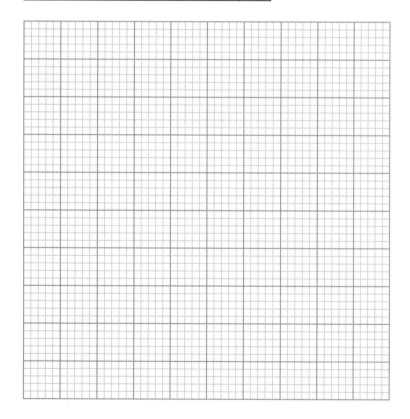

2 Use 1 centimeter on the horizontal axis to represent 5 units. Use 1 centimeter on the vertical axis to represent 10 units.

U	10	5	40	20	25	15	10	20
V	21	91	21	60	50	68	79	59

U	15	35	30	15	20	35	25	30
V	71	31	39	48	62	30	51	38

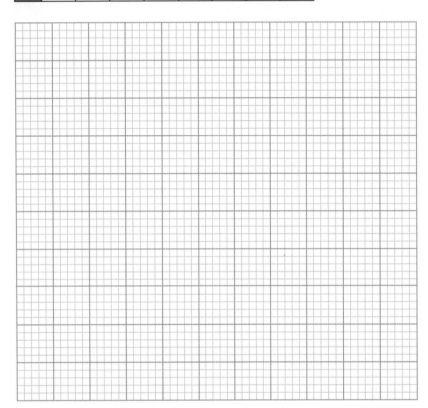

3 Use 1 centimeter on the horizontal axis to represent 10 seconds. Use 1 centimeter on the vertical axis to represent 5 meters per second.

Time (*t* seconds)	40	60	80	20	30	50	70	80
Speed (*v* meters per second)	23	16	13	50	34	19	14	12

Time (*t* seconds)	30	40	70	50	40	70	90
Speed (*v* meters per second)	32	24	15	21	26	16	10

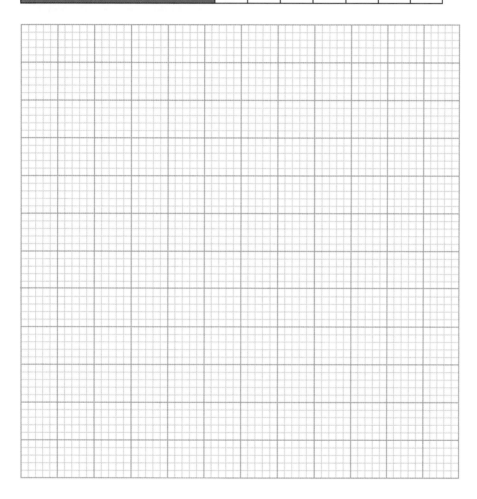

Describe the association between variables *x* and *y* in each scatter plot.

4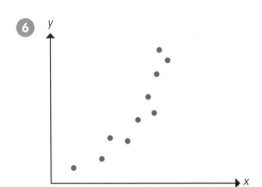

5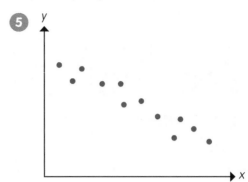

6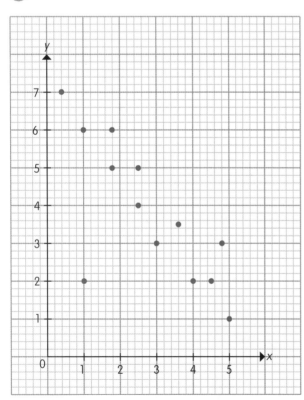

7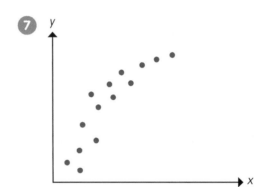

Identify the outlier(s) in the scatter plot.

8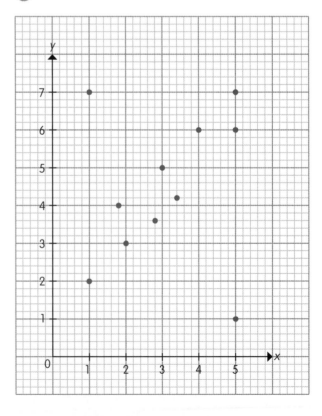

9

Solve

10 The table shows the time spent in batting practice *y* hours, as it relates to the number of games won, *x*, for a softball team over 16 seasons.

Number of Games Won (*x*)	5	3	5	1	1	3	7	3	2	4
Number of Practice Hours (*y* hours)	140	100	150	80	90	120	150	130	90	130

Number of Games Won (*x*)	8	6	2	0	3	6	1	4	5	2
Number of Practice Hours (*y* hours)	160	140	100	90	110	150	160	120	130	110

a Use the graph paper to construct the scatter plot. Use 1 centimeter on the horizontal axis to represent 1 game for the *x* interval from 0 to 10. Use 1 centimeter on the vertical axis to represent 10 hours for the *y* interval from 80 to 160.

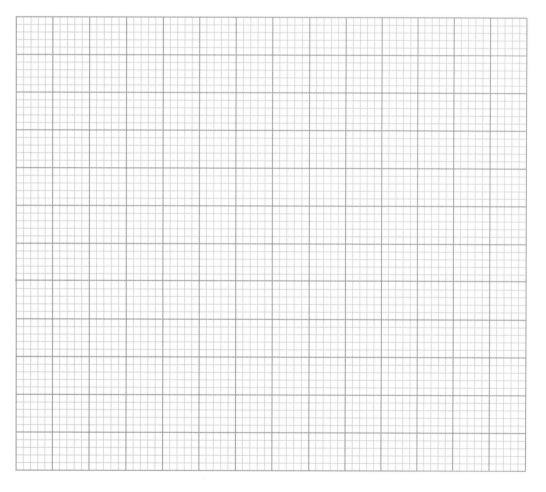

b Identify the outlier. Give a likely explanation for the occurrence of the outlier.

c Describe the association between the number of games won and the number of practice hours. Explain your answer.

11 A teacher instructing a Mathematics course recorded the student scores for a midterm and a final exam.

Midterm Score (*x* points)	34	54	54	80	86	60	42	70	52	85
Final Exam Score (*y* points)	44	66	70	78	42	60	53	68	50	80

Midterm Score (*x* points)	94	38	34	88	47	30	54	75	65	48
Final Exam Score (*y* points)	89	34	41	85	41	36	62	75	64	60

a Use the graph paper to construct the scatter plot. Use 1 centimeter on both axes to represent 10 points.

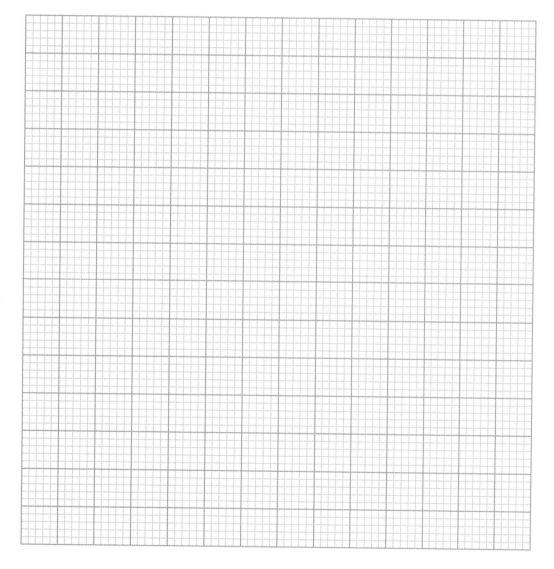

b Identify the outlier. Give a likely explanation of the occurrence of the outlier.

c Describe the association between the points scored on the midterm and those scored on the final exam. Explain your answer.

Chapter 12

Extra Practice and Homework
Statistics

Activity 2   Modeling Linear Associations

State the line that represents a line of best fit for each scatter plot.

1

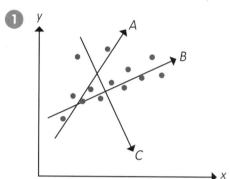

2

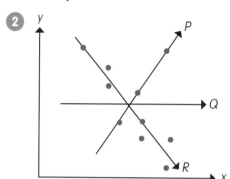

3

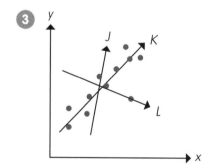

4

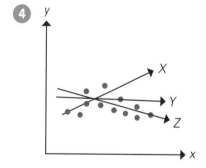

Construct a scatter plot and a line of best fit for the given data.

5 Use 1 centimeter on the horizontal axis to represent 10 units. Use 1 centimeter on the vertical axis to represent 10 units.

U	60	50	70	40	30	60	70	30
V	28	40	20	53	30	31	22	60

U	40	20	30	50	40	80	20
V	48	70	58	44	52	12	72

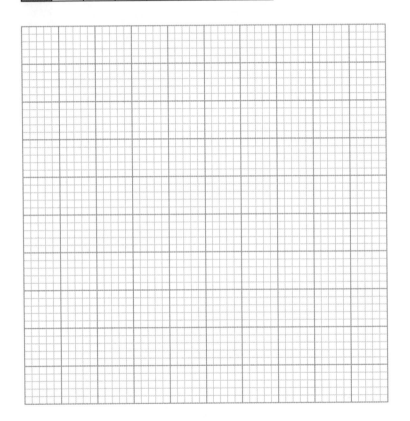

6 Use 1 centimeter on the horizontal axis to represent 1 second. Use 1 centimeter on the vertical axis to represent 10 meters.

Time (*t* seconds)	7	5	4	1	8	3	2	9
Distance (*d* meters)	76	59	51	20	92	40	32	98

Time (*t* seconds)	7	5	4	6	2	3	5
Distance (*d* meters)	82	62	81	72	20	44	58

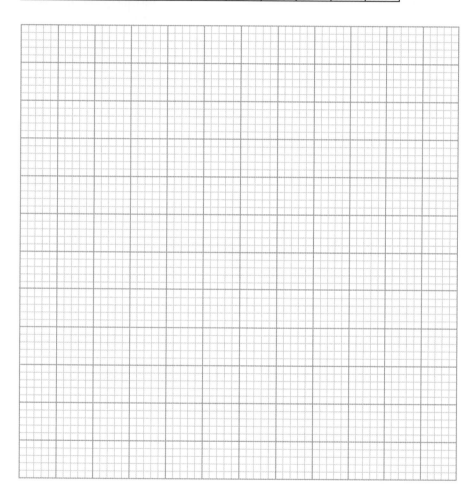

7 Use 1 centimeter on the horizontal axis to represent 1 worker for the *x* interval from 20 to 30. Use 1 centimeter on the vertical axis to represent 10 items produced for the *y* interval from 170 to 280.

Number of Workers (x)	24	23	30	21	28	25	30
Number of Items Produced (y)	210	202	196	176	246	222	274

Number of Workers (x)	27	27	26	23	29	26
Number of Items Produced (y)	270	242	230	198	256	240

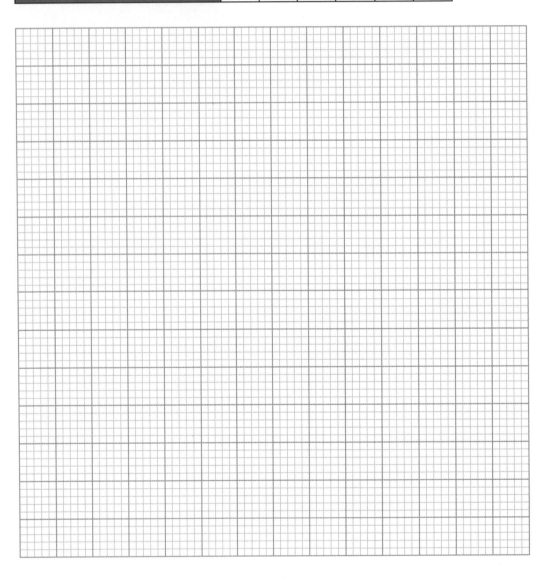

8 Use 1 centimeter on the horizontal axis to represent 1 item for the *x* interval from 50 to 60.
Use 1 centimeter on the vertical axis to represent $5 for the *y* interval from 10 to 50.

Number of Items Assembled (*x*)	53	59	57	50	54	56	51
Cost Per Item (*y* dollars)	40	25	30	50	38	33	48

Number of Items Assembled (*x*)	56	52	55	60	58	55
Cost Per Item (*y* dollars)	32	30	37	18	26	38

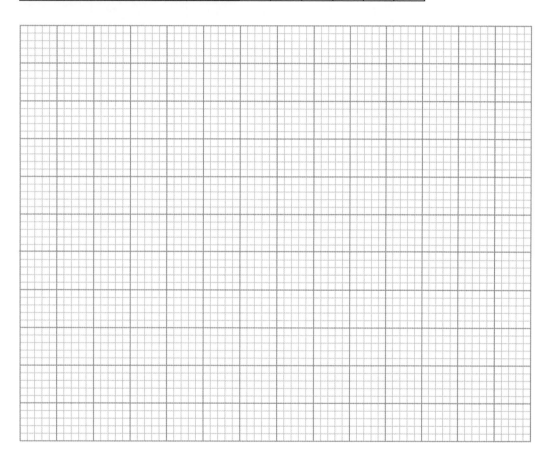

Solve.

9 To understand the relationship between area of living space within a home, *x* square feet, and cost of electricity, *y* dollars, data are collected for a particular month and recorded.

Area of Living Space (*x* square feet)	1,400	1,000	1,300	1,100	1,500	1,300
Electricity Cost (*y* dollars)	210	200	226	206	258	228

Area of Living Space (*x* square feet)	1,200	1,100	1,400	1,200	1,400
Electricity Cost (*y* dollars)	223	212	242	215	246

a Use the graph paper to construct the scatter plot. Use 1 centimeter on the horizontal axis to represent 100 square feet for the *x* interval from 1,000 to 1,500. Use 2 centimeters on the vertical axis to represent $10 for the *y* interval from 200 to 260.

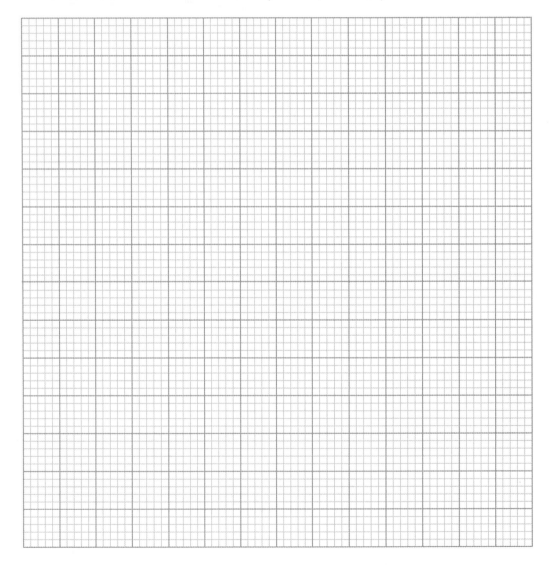

b Sketch a line of best fit.

c Find an equation for the line of best fit.

d Describe the association between area of living space within a home and cost of electricity.

e Identify the outlier. Give a likely explanation of the occurrence of the outlier.

f Use the graph to predict the cost for electricity for a 1,350 square-foot home.

g Use the equation in c to predict the area of living space within a home given an electricity cost of $230.

Chapter 12

Extra Practice and Homework
Statistics

Activity 3 Two-Way Tables

Identify the categorical data.

1 Height, Hobby, Capacity

2 Mass, Velocity, Color

Identify the quantitative data.

3 Brand, Language, Age

4 Length, Name of plants, Shape

State whether the given data is categorical or quantitative.

5 Fast, Moderate, Slow

6 5 points, 15 points, 20 points

Fill in the missing values.

7

a

Fruit

		Apple	Orange	Total
Gender	**Boy**	24	18	_____
	Girl	_____	_____	58
	Total	_____	60	_____

b

Fruit

		Apple	Orange
Gender	**Boy**	_____	0.3
	Girl	0.4	_____
	Total	_____	_____

Solve.

8 A standardized assessment in two subjects, Mathematics and Science, was given to 160 students. Some of the assessment results are shown in the two-way table.

Results for Mathematics

		Pass	Fail	Total
Results for Science	Pass	x	5	125
	Fail	25	y	t
	Total	145	15	160

a Find the number of students who passed both Mathematics and Science, x.

b Find the number of students who failed both Mathematics and Science, y.

c Find the number of students who failed Science, t.

9 A survey was carried out on 30 members of a sports club to find out if they play basketball and volleyball. The results are as follows:

Plays Basketball	B	NB	B	B	NB	B	NB	NB	B	NB	B	NB	NB	B	NB
Plays Volleyball	NV	V	NV	V	V	NV	NV	V	NV	V	V	V	V	NV	V

Plays Basketball	NB	B	B	NB	B	NB	B	NB	B	NB	NB	NB	NB	NB	B
Plays Volleyball	V	NV	NV	V	NV	V	V	V	NV	V	V	NV	V	V	NV

Key: B represents play basketball. NB represents does not play basketball.
V represents play volleyball. NV represents does not play volleyball.

a Construct a two-way table to display the data.

b Which of the following is true? Explain.

- Most of the members play both games.
- Most of the members play one of the two games.
- Most of the members play neither game

c Is there any association between the club members who play basketball and those who play volleyball? Explain.

10 The two-way table shows the type of chess that randomly selected high-school chess club participants play.

Plays International Chess

		Yes	No	Total
Plays Checkers	**Yes**	40	2	42
	No	3	5	8
	Total	43	7	50

a Find the relative frequencies among the rows, and interpret their meanings. Round your answer to the nearest hundredth where necessary.

b Find the relative frequencies within each column, and interpret their meanings. Round your answer to the nearest hundredth where necessary.

c Describe the association between a high-school chess club participant who plays Checkers and one who plays International Chess.

Mathematical Habit **3** **Construct viable arguments**

Carl was given two scatter plots.

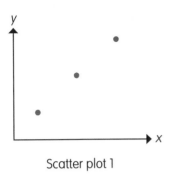

Scatter plot 1

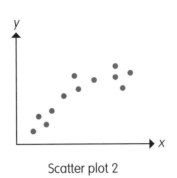

Scatter plot 2

He says that both scatter plots has a positive, strong linear association between the data.
Do you agree? Explain.

Mathematical Habit 2 Use mathematical reasoning

Linda constructs two scatter plots. One displays bivariate data on x and y. The other displays bivariate data on x and z. The equation of the line of best fit for the first scatter plot is $y = x$, and the equation of the line of best fit for the second scatter plot is $z = 3x + 2$. Linda concludes that there is a linear association between y and z. Explain.